Effectiveness of Public-Service Ethics and Good Governance
in the Central Administration of the EU-27

Christoph Demmke / Timo Moilanen

Effectiveness of Public-Service Ethics and Good Governance in the Central Administration of the EU-27

Evaluating Reform Outcomes in the Context of the Financial Crisis

PETER LANG
Frankfurt am Main · Berlin · Bern · Bruxelles · New York · Oxford · Wien

Bibliographic Information published by the Deutsche Nationalbibliothek
The Deutsche Nationalbibliothek lists this publication in the Deutsche Nationalbibliografie; detailed bibliographic data is available in the internet at http://dnb.d-nb.de.

Cover and Photo Design:
© Olaf Gloeckler, Atelier Platen, Friedberg

ISBN 978-3-631-63288-8

www.peterlang.de

CONTENTS

List of Figures

List of Tables

Country Abbreviations

AT	Austria	Republic of Austria
BE	Belgium	Kingdom of Belgium
BG	Bulgaria	Republic of Bulgaria
CY	Cyprus	Republic of Cyprus
CZ	Czech Republic	Czech Republic
DE	Germany	Federal Republic of Germany
DK	Denmark	Kingdom of Denmark
EE	Estonia	Republic of Estonia
EL	Greece	Hellenic Republic
ES	Spain	Kingdom of Spain
FI	Finland	Republic of Finland
FR	France	French Republic
HU	Hungary	Republic of Hungary
IE	Ireland	Ireland
IT	Italy	Italian Republic
LT	Lithuania	Republic of Lithuania
LU	Luxembourg	Grand Duchy of Luxembourg
LV	Latvia	Republic of Latvia
MT	Malta	Republic of Malta
NL	Netherlands	Kingdom of the Netherlands
PL	Poland	Republic of Poland
PT	Portugal	Portuguese Republic
RO	Romania	Romania
SE	Sweden	Kingdom of Sweden
SI	Slovenia	Republic of Slovenia
SK	Slovakia	Slovak Republic
UK	United Kingdom	United Kingdom of Great Britain and Northern Ireland
US/USA		United States of America

European Union Abbreviations

EC	European Commission
EP	European Parliament
ECJ	European Court of Justice

SUMMARY

Over the last two decades, the EU Member States have invested considerable resources in setting ethical standards, as evidenced by the proliferation of ethics codes. However, neither instruments nor methodologies are available for measuring the development of ethical behaviour over long periods of time. There are reasons to believe that, by historical comparisons, civil servants have become more ethically sensitive than before, in such fields as awareness of anti-discrimination, mobbing, gift-taking, political patronage, transparency and accountability. On the other hand, there are many more rules and standards to be broken. Moreover, expectations have risen and standards are becoming ever stricter. New public management reforms also pose new challenges and threats. Overall, ethics policies have become more important. This can be seen in the high level of regulatory activity, growing number of rules and standards, expansion of the meaning of ethics, adoption of more codes of ethics, introduction of more complex accountability mechanisms, growing institutionalisation of ethics (e.g. through the establishment of ethics committees, monitoring bodies, disclosure policies etc.), and more training.

The trend has been towards an increase in the number of rules and standards, as well as the number of issues that are recognised as unethical behaviour. Still, more rules are needed, especially in Eastern Europe while the Nordic countries do not share the same requirement. This is remarkable, as many Eastern European countries already have more rules in place than the Nordic countries. This suggests that more rules are needed in a given political, economic, legal and institutional context characterised by low levels of public trust.

Deregulation of ethics rules seems to be politically impossible and also seems to be lacking support of the general public. However, some countries offer extremely detailed provisions in the field of disclosure of financial interests, which could be simplified. Furthermore, the quality of disclosure legislation could be improved as well. In the meantime, we realise that the trend towards more ethics rules is slowing down. However, our findings do not suggest a shift towards a stronger emphasis on better implementation, enforcement and institutionalisation of ethics policies and rules.

The Member States have invested very little in the evaluation of ethics policies' effectiveness as regards the development of ethical behaviour, costs, bureaucracy and side-effects. However, more Member States are investing in ethics surveys which measure the perception of the ethical climate.

In most countries ethics policies operate in a climate of increasing levels of distrust (higher distrust towards politicians than civil servants). Therefore, the Member States are under pressure to intensify their efforts in the field of ethics to improve public trust. Many other issues, however, may impact the trust levels. It is clear is that doing less would probably decrease the trust levels even further, but doing more, on the other hand, would not necessarily improve public trust.

Ethics policies are mostly scandal-driven. They emerge, flourish, are reformed and expanded as a result of scandals and media attention. Hence, some issues such as corruption and fraud attract a lot of media and political interest, whereas others are not discussed publically to the same extent (e.g., mobbing and disrespect for core values). The fact that ethics policies are often scandal-driven results in the conception of symbolic policies, which at best lead to the adoption of new regulations. Therefore, the focus is on the adoption of new policies, not on the implementation and enforcement of policies. This is confirmed by the fact that ethics is often not taken seriously. The fact that many Member States often do not take ethics seriously contradicts the opinion that civil servants are well aware of ethics rules. Some countries reported also that there was a lack of ethics-related training and awareness. Moreover, ethics training is considered to be as an effective instrument.

As far as the effectiveness of ethics instruments is concerned, leadership and openness are deemed the most effective instruments, followed closely by ethics legislation and ethics training. On the other hand, poor leadership is one of the greatest obstacles in rendering ethics policies effective. Moreover, the findings show that the financial crisis may contribute to a decline in the level of trust placed in leadership. In the view of the present state of implementation, post-employment rules are considered to be the least effective ethics instrument. Strict gift policies, integrity officers, registration of financial interests, protection of whistle-blowers and ethics codes are considered less effective as well.

Most institutional structures are still weak and enforcement and monitoring of ethics policies continues to be an obstacle hindering the establishment of an effective ethics policy. The Member States are much more active in the institutionalisation of anti-corruption policies and conflicts of interest policies than in other ethics-related policies. Overall, institutional structures differ a lot and are highly fragmented. As regards corruption and conflicts of interest policies, one can observe a trend towards the creation of specialised bodies tasked with investigating conflicts of interest and corruption in the national public services. Ideally, these bodies should be independent. Only a few Member States provide for centralised and integrated institutional structures in the field of ethics (e.g., BIOS in the Netherlands, KNAB in Latvia and the Committee on Standards of

Public Life in the United Kingdom). Still, there are more questions than answers concerning effective institutionalisation of ethics policies. What are the experiences so far in monitoring and managing disclosure policies? Have the Member States ever evaluated whether the existing institutional structures existing in the field of ethics are efficient and effective? Are certain coordinating bodies needed? Could advisory bodies such as the Dutch BIOS develop good practices and act as role models? Should all ethics bodies enjoy an institutional and financial autonomy?

An extensive ethics bureaucracy, as can be observed in use in the US and Canada, is not likely to emerge in the near future. However, exceptions exist in the still evolving system of disclosure policies (registers of interests) and in the fight against corruption. The fact that ethics bureaucracies are still limited can be implicitly seen from the fact that the Member States do not consider the costs a problem. More specifically, almost all Member States have no evidence concerning ethics-related spending. This results mainly from the fact that any professional and credible cost evaluation requires a horizontal and integrated approach to cost development. Ethics-related costs are dispersed today amongst many authorities. Another specificity of ethics policies is that the Member States do not perform cost-benefit analyses. Opinions are still prevailing that increasing costs can be justified by the avoidance of ethical scandals.

According to the Member States, the HR reforms that are most vulnerable to integrity violations include recruitment policies, pay reforms, promotion policies and mobility policies. So far, the development of the new ICT is not considered a vulnerable reform trend in relation to ethics. However, the continuing emergence of more diverse ways of communication will raise more ethical challenges in the future. The new ICT also means that individual public servants are going to have access to an ever growing range of communication instruments. On the other hand, opportunities to control the use of ICT and to interfere with privacy issues will be more frequent as well. This means that the public sector will become exponentially more challenging and difficult to manage.

Overall, the impact that the financial crisis has on ethics is neither well researched nor easy to analyse, and most Member States are only beginning to monitor this link. The findings of the study indicate a link between higher budget deficits and higher levels of public distrust. Furthermore, the financial crisis exerts the strongest impact on work place commitment and job satisfaction. Because of the importance of this issue, we recommend it to be monitored more thoroughly in the future.

Other findings suggest that specific attention should be paid to post-employment. Because of the blurring of the boundaries between the public and private sectors, the regulation and management of post-employment will gain in importance in the near future. In addition, the trend towards more flexible forms of employment contracts makes it more difficult to design effective post-employment strategies for the ever more diverse workforce. On the other hand, the Member States have so far been critical as to the effectiveness of post-employment measures. In fact, post-employment is considered as the least effective ethics instrument. Consequently, the Member States should design better instruments in this field.

Finally, we conclude that the emphasis in the field of ethics has been excessively placed on scandals and on preventing wrongdoing. We argue that this regulatory top-down approach to integrity in government must advance beyond the bad person model of law and policy. Instead, we should look at the social psychology of organisational life and at the ability of individuals and leaders to understand and to be critical of their own behaviour.

1. INTRODUCTION: ETHICS AS AN ELEMENT OF GOOD GOVERNANCE

No instruments or methodologies exist to measure the development of ethical behaviour over long periods of time, although there are reasons to believe that, by historical comparisons, civil servants have become more ethically sensitive than before in such fields as awareness of anti-discrimination, mobbing, gift-taking, political patronage, transparency and accountability. Over the last two decades the Member States have also invested considerable resources in setting ethical standards.

All Member States accept that public-service ethics is important for numerous reasons: public institutions protect our countries from external and internal threats. Governments also employ means – such as the threat of violence – that affect the fate of all of us. Public authorities and specific groups of public employees (judges, police officials, military personnel) may interfere with personal rights. Public officials provide means and goods - such as health care, employment opportunities – that are valued by most citizens. Finally, public officials at all governmental levels exercise control over money granted to the government by the Parliament elected by the citizens. It is especially in the times of budgetary constraints that the public service is accountable for the efficient, effective and ethical management of such funds.

Consequently, public officials and public institutions have many opportunities to significantly affect the wellbeing of our societies. Therefore, we want their actions to be guided by rules and policies that prevent them from acting unethically. "Because in a democracy officials and institutions are supposed to act in our name and only on our authority, we want their actions to conform to the moral principles that we share" [1].

As a consequence, for a long time opinions prevailed that civil servants were linked to the authority of the state and could not be compared to other public employees or to the private sector workforce. They were offered a public law status (at least in most states), in order to link them with the state and with the rule of law and not with the interests of individuals. The public law status originates from the French revolution aiming to establish and guarantee a democratic society based on the principles of the French Revolution (Schulze 2004, 39). In Germany the introduction of the public law status was inspired by the philoso-

---

1 Amy Gutmann/Dennis Thompson, Ethics and politics, Thompson/Wadsworth, Fourth Edition, 2006, p.x.

pher Friedrich Hegel. In the Elements of the Philosophy of Right Hegel stated that “the civil [servant's] relationship to his office is not one of contract [...] the civil servant is not employed, like an agent, to perform a single contingent task, but makes this relationship [to his work] the main interest of his spiritual and particular existence [...] But the task which the civil servant has to perform is, in its immediate character, a value in and for itself”[2].

Hegel’s idea of the civil servant and the state as such was conceptualized as a Leviathan which stood above the society and citizens. Its main role was to protect the society by enforcing regulations to achieve fairness and to balance the diverging egoistic interests within the society.

The most influential definition of bureaucracy comes from Max Weber[3]. In his well-known lecture on Politics as a Vocation delivered in 1919, he defined the role of the public officials in the following manner: "The honour of civil servant is vested in his ability to execute conscientiously the order of the superior authorities, exactly as if the order agreed with his own conviction. This holds even if the order appears wrong to him and if, despite the civil servant's remonstrances, the authority insists on the order. Without this moral discipline and self-denial, in the highest sense, the whole apparatus would fall to pieces".

According to Weber, the essence of administrative behaviour is to follow legally given orders. Following this, at a minimal level, administration was considered to be good and ethical if it achieved the implementation and enforcement of the existing laws and policy goals of the Government of the day. Moreover, ethically good or acceptable behaviour was also defined in terms of law obedience, impartiality and standardization. The purpose of rule-orientation was also to achieve fairness and equity, to implement the merit principle, to allocate rights to citizens and to protect public employees against arbitrary administrative decisions. Weber suggested that civil servants should administer without fight, passion and emotion. Communication should be “dehumanised” by eliminating feelings like hate and other irrational and emotional elements. The civil servant should not do the task of a politician: fighting![4] Instead, one of the most important obligations of civil servants is to exercise their functions impartially and rationally.

---

2 Gottfried Hegel, Elements of the philosophy of right, Cambridge University Edition, 1991, pp. 328-336 (§ 287-297).

3 Max Weber, Wirtschaft und Gesellschaft, Volmedia, Paderborn, 1922, pp. 219-227.

4 Max Weber, Politik als Beruf, Reclam, Stuttgart 1999, p. 32.

The principle of the rule of law is definitely one of the core principles in European administrative law, and it is constitutionally guaranteed in every EU Member State. For instance, in Austria and in Finland the principle of the rule of law is explicitly linked to public administration. According to the Austrian constitution, "The entire public administration shall be based on law" (article 18, subsection 1). The Finnish constitution argues that "The exercise of public powers shall be based on an Act. In all public activity, the law shall be strictly observed" (section 2). In the meantime, the notion of good and ethical administration has changed. It has become broader, more complex and more complicated.

Obedience to authority is the cornerstone of the traditional bureaucracy, and this concept is still alive and doing well in many countries. From the ethical point of view, following the law or the superior's orders is usually not problematic. It still is a very relevant guideline for public officials, as it highlights the importance of the rule of law and loyalty to democratically elected government. However, the problem with the Weberian concept is that as an ethical guideline it is simply too narrow for today's multi-level governance.

Today, the level of awareness is growing that work in the public sphere is much more complex and no longer dominated by the principle of rationality as Weber predicted. In fact, today experts are of the opinion that civil servants should not be seen as cogs in the machine. In reality, work in the public sector is more individual, value-laden, emotional, pluralistic and more unpredictable than ever. For example, modern public officials have much more individual decision-making discretion than predicted by Weber. Excessive adherence to rules may be problematic as such as has been illustrated by many authors[5]. On the other hand, the rule of law and administrative law as such remain the core principles of all administrative systems in Europe

Strangely enough, discussions on the importance of (administrative) law and administrative principles did not play a major role during the heyday of New Public Management. One reason for this may be that administrative law was mostly seen as a constraint that blocks policy choices and reform policies. Too much law as such was also seen as suspicious and an underlying reason for public sector inefficiencies. Consequently, traditional administrative behaviour was held to be rigid, rule-bound, centralised and obsessed with dictating how things should be done – regulating the process, controlling the inputs – but totally ig-

---

5 Guy Adams/Danny L. Balfour, In the face of administrative evil: Finding basis for ethics. In Jay M. Shafritz/Albert C. Hyde, Classics of public administration, Sixth Edition, 2008, p. 566; Philip Zimbardo, The Lucifer effect: Understanding how good people turn evil, Random House Trade Paperbacks, 2008.

noring the end results. As a consequence, New Public Management theories were dominated by economic, political and organisational discussions.

In the meantime, the concept of New Public Management has lost a lot of its appeal as the focus on "too much" managerial thinking (and a too strong focus on rational choice theories) is also revealing many negative effects. Therefore, new concepts such as Collaborative Government, Digital Government, Neo-Weberian State or Post-Bureaucratic Government are discussed. Here, the focus is not any more on efficiency and transfer of the private sector model. Instead, it is about the efficiency, effectiveness, coordination, quality and citizen-orientation. In fact, it is all about Good Governance and Good Administration.

Today, the role and limitation of the ethics of neutrality is largely recognised. It is accepted nowadays that individual behaviour is not only determined by rules and policies. Instead, it is also largely influenced by cultural aspects, leadership, fairness perceptions and feelings such as hope, fear, aspirations, etc. Therefore, ethical laws, principles and standards do not cover all areas of human actions, nor do they always help in dealing with ethical dilemmas and personal conflicts. This also suggests that ethically good or acceptable behaviour can be defined not only by focusing on obedience to rules but encompasses also such issues like justice and fairness, leadership, ethical culture and the broader social context of behaviour.

However, given the grand tradition of the "ethics of neutrality", the role and importance of emotions at the workplace is still widely under-researched and, sometimes, not even recognised in the public sector (Cropanzano/Stein/Nadisic 2011: xiii[6]). Changing behaviours and people is also more than difficult and cannot be accomplished by a simple introduction of new rules, standards and policies. Or, as Follett noted in The Giving of Orders[7], you "cannot get people to do things most satisfactorily by ordering them or exhorting them; but also that even reasoning with them, even convincing them intellectually, may not be enough (…) For all our past life, our early training, our later experience, all our emotions, beliefs, prejudices, every desire that we have, have formed certain habits of mind … Therefore it will do little good merely to get intellectual agreement; unless you change the habit pattern of people, you have not really changed your people"[8].

---

6 Russel Cropanzano/Jorgan H. Stein/Thierry Nadisc, Social justice and the experience of emotion, Routledge, New York, 2011.

7 Mary Parker Follett, The giving of orders, in Shafritz/Hyde, op. cit., p. 65.

8 Ibid.

Today, the concept of good administration and good governance is replacing the talk of New Public Management (NPM). Although there are just as many definitions of Good Governance as there are of NPM, the concept of Good Governance includes broader and varied political and organisational principles of management practices. Good governance is also about good leadership, organisational fairness, non-discrimination and an ever increasing set of issues which are considered unethical.

Figure 1. Characteristics of good governance[9]

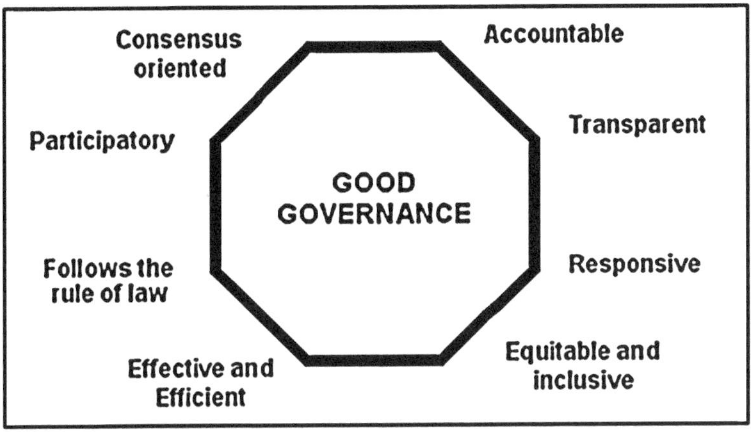

Whereas efficient government is more about a balanced ratio between input, outputs and outcomes, effective government is about better solutions to problems and challenges (higher health standards, fighting unemployment, reducing environmental pollution), and about higher quality levels (better services for citizens). Good and ethical government is about being good and maintaining and achieving societal standards (democracy, trust, respect, integrity, civility etc.). Can governance accomplish both? Is doing good the same thing as doing the things right? Can government be effective, efficient and good?

Still, especially the rhetoric of good government is full of good but also conflicting intentions. We want better governance, better leadership, representative and diverse administrations, more flexibility, less hierarchy, more job autonomy, participatory management, effective anti-discrimination rules, more perform-

9 United Nations Economic and Social Commission for Asia and the Pacific, What is good governance? See http://www.unescap.org/pdd/prs/ProjectActivities/Ongoing/gg/governance.asp, last time checked on 26.3.2012.

ance, better accountability structures, more transparency, more openness and more citizen-orientation. Consequently, in discussions on good governance, the following factors are frequently mentioned: accountability, transparency, combating corruption and participatory governance[10].

In fact, the concept of good governance and good administration is becoming broader and broader and includes different things such as the call for less administrative burdens, better quality of services, higher levels of citizen satisfaction, more transparency while enhancing efficiency and levels of public trust. Likewise, ethical government is also becoming more complex and expanded from an early focus on anti-corruption and fraud to many other fields, including conflicts of interest, ethical leadership, transparency, accountability, disclosure policies, post-employment etc.

Thus, ethics policies share a number of features with the field of anti-discrimination (and/or diversity). Whereas in the past the concept of anti-discrimination focused on equal opportunities, equal treatment and equal pay, today it encompasses a much wider field and includes the fight against discrimination based on sex, racial or ethnic origin, religion or belief, disability, age or sexual orientation (Art. 10 TFEU). The case law of the EJE in the field of age discrimination includes an impressive number of important and complex judgements.

According to Salminen, we are moving from a minimalist concept to a maximalist concept of good and ethical governance[11]. Salminen argues that the "minimalist concept involves the minimum requirements for ethically acceptable governance, whereas the maximalist concept aims at enriching our understanding of what ethically good and high quality governance involves or could involve. The minimalist concept of ethical governance states absolute prohibitions that public authorities and civil servants are forbidden to violate in all circumstances. They include prohibitions of all forms of corruption (e.g., bribery, graft, and nepotism), extortion and coercion, deception, theft, and discrimination (….). The maximal concept of ethical governance additionally invokes positive commands, such as 'Be fair and impartial', 'Safeguard the well-being of citizens', and 'Take good care of the administrative tasks entrusted to you'. Furthermore, the maxi-

---

10 Sam Agere, Promoting good governance. Principles, practices and perspectives. Commonwealth Secretariat, 2000.

11 Ari Salminen (Ed.), Ethical governance, University of Vaasa, 2010, p. 32.

malist concept specifies positive characteristics of a good authority or civil servant, such as diligence, kindness, patience, and humaneness"[12].

This study is about the question whether the move towards a new and more complex concept of ethics and governance is effective. Is it better than the traditional concept of the "neutrality of ethics"? Is ethical behaviour improving? Are newly designed instruments effective? Or, perhaps we are expecting too much? Are we becoming too demanding? Is it possible to have too much ethics?

As we will see throughout this study, we cannot offer a ten-steps-to-success handbook. However, we will try to analyse the existing challenges as thoroughly as possible. This study presents an overview of ethics policies' effectiveness on central administrative level, the main reform trends and the main outcomes of selected national reform policies in the field of ethics. The overall aim of this work is to provide empirical evidence, facts and comparative statistical evidence in order to help experts and scholars better understand the nature of reforms and the changes that are taking place. This alone is risky business, since ethics policies are very complex and technical. Thus, any comparative study faces the risk of being far too superficial. Hence, this study relates to basic research which may be considered a good point of departure for a more specific study of the different instruments and issues, such as those related to leadership, post-employment and whistle blowing issues

We would like to thank the Polish EU Presidency and all national and European experts within the European Network of Public Administration[13] for their vital contribution to this study. We are also grateful to Krzysztof Banaś, the HRWG Chair for his consistent support throughout the entire project, and Councellor Katarzyna Dudzik for her excellent coordinating skills and diligent help.

---

12 Ibid.

13 For more information about the network, see http://www.eupan.eu/, last time checked 26.3.2012.

2. METHODOLOGY

2.1 Research question and work assignment

Any honest dialogue about ethics and good governance requires the ability to communicate difficult issues and the courage to bring out sometimes dissenting opinions. It is well known that public-service ethics is considered to be a very serious problem in some countries, whereas it is considered less problematic in others. This presents an important challenge for a comparative study since many of the issues it discusses are complex and sensitive. Consequently, governments, organisations and even national experts often shy away from discussing them openly. In fact, this study can only look at ethics and good governance policies as critically, openly and honestly as possible. There are no easy answers. However, as this study hopefully shows, there are some promising answers and many – surprising – results.

Comparative studies on public-service ethics on central governmental level in the EU Member States have a rather recent history[14]. However, studies on public sector ethics and integrity started earlier in the OECD-world[15]. Moreover, the first international comparative study on local integrity systems, which is paying attention to the policies, practices and actors at the local government level, was published by Anechiarico, Huberts and Six[16].

---

14 Danielle Bossaert/Christoph Demmke, Main challenges in the field of ethics and integrity in the EU Member States, EIPA, Maastricht, 2005; Christoph Demmke/Mark Bovens/Thomas Henökl/Timo Moilanen, Regulating conflicts of interest for holders of public office in the European Union, EIPA, Maastricht, 2008; Christoph Demmke/Thomas Henökl/Timo Moilanen, What are public services good at? Success of public services in the field of human resource management, Report to the 50th Meeting of the Directors-General of Public Services of the Member States of the European Union, May 2008. Finally, a study on improving trust in government was carried out in 2009 within the informal settings of the European Social Dialogue for central public administrations by David Tarren, Improving trust in central government, A report for TUNED and EUPAN, 2009.

15 The OECD has published a number of studies on integrity, fight against corruption and conflict of interests. For example, OECD, Trust in government: Ethics measures in OECD countries, Paris 2000; OECD, Public sector integrity: A framework for assessment, Paris 2005.

16 Frank Anechiarico/Leo Huberts/Frederique Six, Local integrity systems: World cities fighting corruption and safeguarding integrity, Boom, Amsterdam, 2008.

Surprisingly, only few studies discuss the institutionalisation of ethics and the effectiveness of ethics and integrity measures as such[17]. For many years, discussions about public-service ethics have been relatively abstract and theoretical, while focussing on principles and obligations such as the duty of employees to be impartial and to obey the law. At the same time, governments' ethics policies have focused on the input side, e.g. introduction of new rules, standards, codes and other ethics instruments. Later on, discussions concentrated on the effects of new public management reforms on ethics. Often, these discussions have had an ideological tone as many experts offered explanations about tensions between public and private sector values. Consequently, the argument was that New Public Management would lead to more ethical challenges[18].

Until today, only few discussions took place on the "output" and "outcome" side and the impact of reform policies on workplace behaviour, as well as on the added-value and the effectiveness of ethics policies. Also cost-benefit tests of ethics policies have only rarely been carried out. Moreover, there is very little research on the organisational aspects of ethics. How can ethics policies be institutionalised effective within an organisation? What do we know about good practices and best ways to organise ethics policies?[19]

With the coming of the financial crisis, ongoing restructuring processes are taking place within European economies. Voluntary and involuntary redundancy, reform of retirement schemes, workplace transfers and the reduction of salaries not only affect public sector and public service employees, but exert an impact on workplace ethics as well.

In our study, we move one step forward in the discussions about the effectiveness of ethics policies. Our argument is that discussions about ethics should be better integrated with other policy areas which have a direct effect on the behaviour of employees. These include e.g. public management reforms, impact of the financial crisis on the behaviour of employees, importance of HR policies and leadership styles, relationship between perceptions of organisational fairness and organisational culture and employees' attitudes, as well as cost and benefits con-

---

17 Alain Hoekstra/Leo Kaptein/D. van de Burg, Het institutionaliseren van integriteit: de organisatie van de integriteitsfunctie binnen lokale overheden verkend. In Bestuurswetenschappen, no. 5/2010, pp. 54-73.

18 H. George Frederickson/Richard K. Ghere (Eds.), Ethics in public management, Sharpe, New York, 2005.

19 Dennis F. Thompson, Restoring responsibility: Ethics in government, business, and healthcare. Cambridge University Press, 2004.

sideration. We propose to have a broader discussion on the added-value of good governance policies, including ethics policies and ethics instruments.

Ethics is an integral element of good governance. Both concepts share a number of common features. Generally speaking, good governance policies should aim at more citizen orientation, transparency, accountability, anti-discrimination, fight against corruption, and participation So far, the effects of good governance policies have mostly been evaluated positively. Why should one be against transparency, participation, openness etc.? Little effort has been devoted, however, to discussions on the more problematic aspects of the good governance concept. For example, does more transparency lead to more intrusion into privacy? How bureaucratic are anti-discrimination policies? Last but not least, how effective are ethics policies? Do more rules and standards in the field of corruption and conflict of interest reduce the scale of corruption and prevent the conflict of interest situations?

The positive intention of the good governance concept may also conflict with the harsh reality of austerity measures which are implemented in many countries. How are public employees affected by these changes? Surprisingly, so far only few evaluations have been conducted regarding the effects of austerity policies on the quality of services, ethical behaviour, motivation, commitment and performance of public employees.

In April 2011, the Chancellery of the Prime Minister of the Polish EU Presidency commissioned the European Institute of Public Administration to undertake the present study. According to the mandate given by the Polish Presidency, the purpose of this study was to analyse and compare the effectiveness of various policies, rules and standards of professional ethics in the field of good governance among the EU Member States. Another point of interest was to collect more information on the costs and benefits of ethics policies. The Member States were invited to contribute to the study through their input, discussions and workshops, and finally discussions on the top-administrative level held by the Directors-General during their 57th meeting in December 2011 in Warsaw. All Member States and the European Commission contributed to the study.

2.2 Methodology and hypothesis

Today, discussions on good governance policies focus on the positive effects as well (and much less on the negative or unintentional effects), although there is ample evidence that many good governance policies are also paradoxical. For example, while people call for less administrative burdens, administrative simplification and deregulation, they are also asking for new laws and rules in data protection, climate change, corruption, conflicts of interests, citizen rights, anti-discrimination, diversity and the fight against terrorism. Another paradoxical feature of the current reform discussion is the discrepancy between the reform pace in some areas and its lack in other spheres. For example, whereas the introduction of new ethics policies and accountability mechanisms is high on the agenda, the evaluation of the effectiveness of ethics and accountability instruments has been neglected.

The history of public management reforms is also a history of tradeoffs, limits, dilemmas, paradoxes and contradictions[20]. In their seminal book Public Management Reform, Pollitt and Bouckaert illustrate the following contradictions[21]:

- Increase political control of the bureaucracy/free managers to manage/empower service consumers
- Give priority to making savings/improve the quality of the public sector
- Promote flexibility and innovation/increase citizen trust and therefore governmental legitimacy
- Motivate staff and promote cultural change/weaken tenure and downsize
- Reduce burden of internal scrutiny and associated paperwork/sharpen managerial accountability
- Develop more partnerships and contracting out/improve horizontal coordination
- Increase effectiveness/sharpen managerial accountability
- Promote open government and transparency/protect privacy

The new values are not free of contradictions. During the era when treating everybody equally meant treating everybody fairly is not anymore the paradigm of our times: "The age of standardization and the decline of patronage government were well suited for the belief in and practice that equal treatment for all is fair treatment. Postmodern societies along with ethnic, racial, gender, and age diversity have challenged elected officials and administrators around the world to rethink how to treat people unequally and yet to be fair"[22]. In the field of public service reforms this is one of the biggest challenges as new ways of conceptualizing merit and fairness are also creating new dilemmas, flaws and fairness issues. One example is the abandonment of a standardized seniority-based pay system in many Member States. Today, these systems are seen as being in con-

---

20 Christopher Pollitt/Geert Bouckaert, Public management reform: A comparative analysis, third edition, Oxford, 2011, p. 182.

21 Ibid., p. 187.

22 Donald Menzel, Ethics and integrity in the public service. In Donald Menzel/Harvey L. White (Eds.), The state of public administration, Sharpe, London, 2011, p. 122.

flict with our modern understanding of merit and fairness. In addition, the case law of the European Court of Justice is addressing the question whether seniority-based pay systems are in conflict with the principle of anti-discrimination in the field of age[23].

Today, the Member States of the European Union have become more meritocratic and, at the same time, more polarized. The more the concept of meritocracy is becoming a reality, the more it seems to legitimate a hierarchy of privilege[24]. The paradox with the principle of meritocracy lies with the problem that our systems, which reward talented people, leave no hiding place for those who do not succeed in the competitive struggle. Today, rising levels of inequality and problems with social mobility can lead to a loss of social capital, frustration, discontentment and alienation. "A further serious deficiency in the ethical grounds of meritocracy is its virtual absence of discourse on what areas of "merit does not do justice to vast differences in status, reward and power ..."[25]. Another problem is that the principle of meritocracy can, at times, be self-defeating, "The more opportunity there is for people to succeed in society, the less value such success is likely to have for them"[26]. If all people invest in more and better education and invest in their competences and skills, the process ends as a race to the top. Everybody is likely to become disappointed quickly. Robert Merton showed that career satisfaction was higher in those units in which the promotion rates were low, than in those with high ones. "If there is one thing worse than being blocked, it is seeing others succeed where you have failed"[27]. Merit, as the basis for employment decisions, is one of the core values. Yet employee faith in the application of merit principle is relatively low and appears to be in decline in many countries. "Even allowing for the fact that perceptions vary according to whether respondents were successful in obtaining a job, the results are still unsatisfactory"[28].

The process of attaching more importance to individual values and merit-based approaches can be also seen in other fields. For example, recruitment proce-

---

23 See the ECJ cases C-17/05 (Cadman), C-184/89 (Nimz), C-243/93 (Hill and Stapleton), C-109/88 (Danfoss), C-297/10/298/10 (Hennigs vs. Eisenbahn (C-297/10) and C-298/10 (Bundesamt and Land Berlin vs Alexander Mai).

24 Donald Menzel, Ethics and integrity in the public service. In Menzel/White, op. cit., p. 137.

25 Ibid., p. 131.

26 Georg Dench (Ed.), The rise and rise of meritocracy, Blackwell, Oxford, 2006, p. 190.

27 Ibid.

28 Lynelle Briggs, Testing APS ethics: Where's the integrity?, In: The Australian Journal of Public Administration, Vol. 68, No. 2/2009, p. 134.

dures, mobility policies, pay and promotion mechanisms are constantly being reformed as a consequence of new de-standardised and individualised fairness and merit conceptions. Moreover, attitudes towards the principle of seniority, the importance of qualifications, skills and competences have changed and become more flexible and individualised. Overall, most countries follow trends towards decentralization of HR responsibilities and different public sector organisations promote different values. One should expect that this development towards the fragmentation and diversification of the public services has also important effects on the diversification of values and ethics policies.

In reality, ethics and good governance policies can have many more effects, although most discussions have mainly focused on the positive effects, and much less on the negative effects or unintentional side-effects. For example, the prohibition of alcohol in the USA early in the last century was a moral as well as law enforcement fiasco, but this is not the case with the recent anti-smoking policies. Smoking rates have been on a decline for a number of years now in industrialised countries.

Until recently, transparency was seen as an area with entirely positive effects. Citizens and media demand greater transparency from governments and require detailed information on the who, why and how of decision-making. Transparency is seen as essential in holding governments accountable, maintaining confidence in public institutions and supporting a level playing field for businesses. Greater transparency is also key to upholding integrity in the public sector by reducing the risk of fraud, corruption and mismanagement of public funds[29]. Whereas open government webpages such as 'www.data.gov' and reports from international organisations[30] applaud the benefits of more transparency, other authors arrive at very ambivalent conclusions as to the effects of transparency policies[31]. For example, the requirement to submit detailed personal data and information to various types of registers can hurt an individual's sense of integrity[32]. In 2010, the Wikileaks scandal showed in extreme how the quest for

29 OECD, Government at a glance, Paris 2011.

30 World Bank Institute, Proactive transparency: The future of the right to information?, Washington D.C., 2011.

31 Christopher Hood/David Heald (Eds.), *Transparency. The key to better governance?* Oxford University Press, 2006; David Brin, The transparent society, Perseus Books, Cambridge M.A., 1998.

32 Also a SIGMA report states that "nonetheless, experience in OECD and EU countries has shown that promoting openness in government and administration in practice is a very difficult task. Ensuring the right to know of citizens through appropriate access to information stored in public offices remains an elusive policy goal. The need to pre-

openness and transparency may clash with other political and administrative principles.

Hesse et al. have presented a useful matrix to assess various effects the reform may have[33]. Firstly, the impact of reform measures on major goal achievements can be positively or negatively effective or ineffective. Secondly, reforms may have an impact not only on the main goal but also on some other goals. In other words, they may have positive or negative side-effects, or they may not have side-effects at all. From these combinations it is possible to construct a nine-fold table describing nine different effect combinations (Table 1). Applying this analytic framework to the field of ethics may also help to encourage a more rational discourse.

Table 1. Nine possible effects of public sector reforms

	Impact on other goals		
Impact on major goal	**None** (no side-effects)	**Positive side-effects**	**Negative side-effects**
Positively effective main goal achieved	(1) *Simple effectiveness* (operation according to plan)	(2) *Effectiveness with a bonus* (objective reached with reinforcement of other goals)	(3) *Effectiveness plus jeopardy* (objective reached with some sacrifice of other goals)
Ineffective no effect	(4) *Simple futility* (e.g. "all talk and no action" in reform programmes)	(5) *Futility but with a bonus* (main target untouched but positive side-effects)	(6) *Futility plus jeopardy* (main target untouched but negative side-effects)
Negatively effective reverse effects	(7) *Simple perversity* (outcome the very opposite of the aim)	(8) *Perversity but with a bonus* (perverse effects on target but positive effect elsewhere)	(9) *Perversity plus jeopardy* (perverse effect on target plus other negative effects)

serve primary public and private interests (from confidentiality of international relations to privacy of individuals) is difficult to reconcile with the quest for transparency in concrete cases". OECD-SIGMA, The right to open public administrations in Europe, Sigma paper no. 46, Paris 2010, p. 3.

33 Joachim Hesse/Christopher Hood/Guy Peters (Eds.), Paradoxes in public sector reform: An international comparison, Duncker & Humblot, Berlin 2003.

Our main hypothesis in this study is that the present reform trends in the field of ethics have a number of positive effects, but they also have negative, mostly unintentional side-effects, such as more bureaucracy, higher costs, more intrusion into privacy, moral instruments for media and political purposes, less instead of more public trust etc. Moreover, the effects of more rules and standards depend on other variables, such as good working conditions, good leadership and perception of fair HR policies. Another hypothesis is that many Member States have become very active in the field of public-service ethics. They assume that ethics policies are important, that many more rules and policies have been introduced, that leadership is an important instrument in the field of ethics, that investments have been made in training policies, that public officials are very cognisant in the field of ethics etc. Still, we experience that in administrative reality, ethics policies are not taken seriously and there is a gap between political and media activism and the effective institutionalisation of ethics policies. Our final hypothesis concerns the effects of many management reforms and the impact of the financial crisis. We believe that many ongoing reforms, mostly those which are implemented within the framework of austerity policies, have highly ambivalent effects on workplace behaviour.

2.3 Studying the effects of public management and organisational reforms on ethics

For many years, researchers have attempted to find out why employees behave ethically or unethically in the workplace[34]. Most have accepted the distinction offered by Kish-Gephart et al.[35] as to the influence of individual characteristics, moral issue characteristics and organisational characteristics. Especially the social environment in which public employees operate has been shown to relate to important output variables. Consequently, it is important to analyse whether particular dimensions of the organisational and social context have connections with the attitude and behaviour of the individual employees. For example, employees' perceptions of ethical climate, ethical culture and leadership styles have been related to employees' attitudes and behaviour. More theoretically, the equity theory claims that (public) employees compare their input to the organisa-

34 J. Bernerth/Jack Walker/F. Walter/RR. Hirschfeld, A study of workplace justice. Differences during times of change: It is not all about me, in: The Journal of Applied Behavioural Science, Vol. 47, No. 3/2011, pp. 336-36-359; P. Zoghbi-Manrique-de-Lara, Do unfair procedures predict employees ethical behavior by deactivating formal regulations?, in: Journal of Business Ethics, Vol. 94, No. 3/2010, pp. 411-425.

35 JJ. Kish-Gephart/D.A Harrison/L.K. Treviño (2010), Bad apples, bad cases, and bad barrels: Meta-analytic evidence about sources of unethical decisions at work, in: Journal of Applied Psychology, Vol. 95, No. 1/2010, pp. 1-31.

tion (effort, stress, intelligence, work intensity) with what they get out of this input (pay, rewards, promotion, status etc.). They also compare this with the input/output ratio of their colleagues. The equity theory is related to the theories of social justice, behavioural ethics and merit. We will address them later on in this study. If public employees are not satisfied, inequity may be experienced which can result in dissatisfaction or demotivation or other behavioural effects. Today, the introduction of austerity measures changes the input/output ratio. However, so far, little is known as to the effects of these measures on feelings of inequity.

In his prominent book A Theory of Justice, philosopher John Rawls argues for a principled reconciliation of liberty and equality[36]. Rawls argues that inequality is acceptable only if it is to the advantage of those who are worst-off. Rawls develops two principles of fairness and justice. According to the first principle of justice, each person is to have an equal right to the most extensive basic liberty compatible with a similar liberty for others. The basic liberties of citizens are, roughly speaking, political liberty (i.e. the right to vote and run for office), freedom of speech and assembly, liberty of conscience, freedom of personal property and freedom from arbitrary arrest. According to the second principle of justice, social and economic inequalities are to be arranged so that (a) they are to be of the greatest benefit to the least-advantaged members of society (the difference principle) and (b) offices and positions must be open to everyone under conditions of fair equality of opportunity[37].The first principle may not be violated, even for the sake of the second principle, above an unspecified but low level of economic development. It is, under most conditions, lexically prior to the second principle. However, because various basic liberties may conflict, it may be necessary to trade them off against each other for the sake of obtaining the largest possible system of rights. There is thus some uncertainty as to exactly what is mandated by the principle, and it is possible that a plurality of sets of liberties satisfy its requirements.

Today, all EU Member States are, broadly, meritocratic countries which subscribe to the Rawlsian principles. On the other hand, the ever stronger focus on performance and merit has also produced more inequalities in our society (OECD 2008)[38].

The term organisational justice refers to the extent at which administrative reforms and HR policies are perceived as fair in their outcome. Organisational jus-

---

36 John Rawls, A theory of justice, Harvard University Press, 1971.

37 Ibid., p. 303.

38 OECD, Growing unequal?, Paris, 2008; OECD, Divided we stand: Why inequality keeps rising?, Paris 2011.

tice theories have also been linked to health issues. Experts often make a distinction between distributive justice, procedural justice and interactional justice[39]. Distributive justice refers to the fairness of the allocation of outcomes. For example, "my unit's head applies the same performance assessment conditions as the employees do, and the outcomes we get are fair and correspond to our performance". Procedural justice refers to the fairness of the decision-making procedure behind the allocation of these outcomes. For instance, "my unit's head is fair and consistent in the procedures she/he uses, and I have the opportunity to express my view during the feedback procedures". Interactional justice pertains to the fairness of treatment throughout the process of decision-making and allocating outcomes. For example, "I am treated with respect, and the procedures applicable in the performance assessment have been explained in a timely manner and the explanations given in the feedback are seen reasonable". In their study on performance appraisal systems, Kim and Rubianty conclude that their findings "support the existence of distributive, procedural and interactional fairness of performance appraisals and their positive associations with intrinsic motivation"[40].

The impact of organisational justice perceptions on performance had its origin in the equity theory. This suggests that when people suffer from injustice, they seek to re-establish justice somewhere else (for example by changing their level of job performance). Procedural justice affects performance as a result of work processes and their impact on employee attitudes, whereas distributive justice affects performance when efficiency issues are involved (for example the distribution of bonuses after performance assessments). The conclusion of this theory is that improving justice perceptions also improves motivation, productivity and performance.

Therefore, not only law and principles, but also fairness perceptions can strongly influence the individual behaviour and may exert a good or a bad impact on individual and organisational performance. For example, as we will see later on in this study, job satisfaction is negatively related with the introduction of austerity measures (and the perceived perceptions of lower levels of organisational justice. In addition, organisational commitment seems to be related to perceptions of procedural and distributional justice which are, again, related to measures taken in the context of the financial crisis).

---

39 Seok Eun Kim/Dian Rubianty, Perceived fairness of performance appraisals in the federal government: Does it matter?, in: Review of Public Personnel Administration, Vol. 31, No. 4/2011, pp. 329-349.

40 Ibid., p. 344.

Thus, people are naturally attentive to the justice of events and situations in their everyday lives, across a variety of contexts. Individuals react to actions and decisions made by organisations every day. In the academic literature, experts have pointed to many negative effects that unprofessional performance assessments, job terminations, unfair promotion decisions, decisions not based on merit but personal considerations, salary cuts, unfair recruitment decisions, etc. have had on fairness perceptions. In fact, the present trend is characterised by the introduction of different austerity measures in many EU countries. What then happens to employees if national governments continue to introduce harsh pay cuts and pension reforms, decide on voluntary or obligatory job transfers, limit promotions, relax job security, reduce the scope of health schemes, reform the standard employment model, etc.?

The financial crisis has also accelerated reforms of the traditional employment status (lifetime tenure, full-time employment) and the flexicurity agenda. More Member States are confronted with growing inconsistencies regarding the employment of public employees in civil service positions. More Member States also employ a growing number of fixed-term employees. This has led to the fact that several Member States apply different employment relationships in the same sectors and sometimes for the same professions. Here, little is known on the ethical behaviour of civil servants, public employees and employees under short-term contracts. Do the different categories of staff show different behaviour patterns because of different employment statuses?

Economic pressures, budgetary cuts, the reduction in salaries and promotion opportunities may result in more stress, competition and a general decline in organisational culture (ethical climate). In these situations issues such as fairness, courtesy, abuse of power and impartiality may be at risk. This again can result in more ethical violations, such as stealing organisational resources, misconduct at work, unwelcome behaviour etc.

Still, there is very little evidence so far on the impact of the financial crisis on workplace behaviour as such. For example, compensation and benefit reductions and adjusted work schedules, which have a direct impact on an employee's personal finances, life, and livelihood, are most likely linked to increases in misconduct, disengagement and weaker work commitment. One particular area of concern for management is whether and how employees "act out" against the organisation in response. A recent US study[41] shows that many forms of misconduct seem to demonstrate employees' attempts to take out their frustrations and/or reclaim some of what they lost as a result of management decisions. For example, in compensation/benefit reduction situations, there is an 81 per cent rise in Internet abuse and an 84 per cent increase in company resource abuse. In contrast, layoffs are associated with lower rises (38 per cent and 52 per cent, respectively) in different forms of misconduct. Cost-cutting reforms are also linked to greatly reduced rates of employee commitment and to disengagement (Gallup), which has been linked to employee performance and engagement. However, the financial crisis may also have positive effects or no effect at all on public-service ethics. For example, it is also possible that during hard times, when an organisation's well-being or even existence may be at risk, the management talks more about the importance of high standards in order to guide the organisation through the crisis. It may also be that some are less inclined to commit misconduct when management is on high alert.

2.4 Limitations of the study

Because of the comparative and empirical approach of this study, the authors are well aware of the many difficulties and challenges involved in performing this study. To this should be added the fact that public-service ethics is a highly sensitive and even political issue in times of a deep economic crisis that many Member States are facing. The fact that all 27 Member States and the European Commission contributed to the study, confirms the great degree of interest in this subject. A number of limitations should be taken into account when interpreting our findings, however. The first limitation concerns the approach. This study does not focus on corruption and the fight against corruption. Although anti-corruption measures are related to ethics measures, we have decided to focus on administrative ethics. Another reason was the need to avoid repeating the already accomplished studies by other international organisations such as OECD, World Bank and the Council of Europe (GRECO).

Also, in the field of ethics we can only discuss and analyse what "we see". In fact, ethics resembles an iceberg and we only can see the top of it. In Objective Knowledge, Karl Popper distinguished between predictable, rational, machine-

---

41 Ethics resource center, National business ethics survey 2009: Saving the company comes at a cost, 2010. See http://www.ethics.org/nbes/files/NBESResearchBrief.pdf, last time checked on 26.3.2012.

like orderly social systems and social systems that are like clouds[42]. Studying ethics belongs to those systems that are like clouds - fuzzy, complex and fluid.

As already discussed, ethics reforms and policies in the public services constitute many legal, economic and political reforms that have cultural, psychological and behavioural effects. Appiah illustrates how moral upheaval is motivated by disregard, the violation of honour codes and the lack of respect rather than by learned principles and virtues[43].

Consequently, public-service ethics have also become more complex. One of the greatest strengths of research in the field of public sector ethics lies in the diversity of those who are interested in the topic. Where else could we find more management scholars, public administration experts, psychologists, political scientists, moral philosophers, organisational sociologists and behavioural economists? In the meantime, this literature covers a wide array of fields ranging from the design of ethics infrastructure to workplace ethics.

Other difficulties are that the factors of explanation are multiple and that they are found simultaneously at the individual level (problems with handling money, profession-related problems, dubious social contacts, etc.), at the organisational level of the public sector (bad leadership, unfair HRM decisions, insufficient preventive measures, low salaries, etc.) and at the political/economic level (no clear distinction between the executive and judiciary, etc.). The best solution is to perform research concerning the link between ethics and trust levels. In this study we will explain why studying trust requires a much more complex approach.

Such complexity must of course also be taken into account when determining the effectiveness of ethics policies and ethics instruments. Unethical behaviour is not attributed mainly to a few dishonest individuals. Ethical behaviour of public officials depends, to a large extent, on the organisational, institutional and legal features in place. According to this assumption, breaches of integrity are primarily a consequence of the negative impact of specific opportunity and motivation structures, such as the lack of efficient awareness and control mechanisms, bad working conditions, low civil service ethos, or simply the fact that the chance of being caught is rather small.

---

42 Karl Popper, Objective knowledge, Oxford University Press, 1972.

43 Kwame Anthony Appiah, Eine Frage der Ehre oder Wie es moralischen Revolution kommt. C.H.Beck, Munchen, 2011.

The relevant literature illustrates very well that proper behaviour in the public sector not only depends on one single instrument such as an effective disciplinary legislation, setting-up of efficient control and monitoring bodies, or an attractive code of conduct, but more widely on the existence of an overall national integrity system (Transparency International), or multipronged anti-corruption strategy (World Bank, GRECO), or a multidimensional ethics infrastructure (OECD). The main characteristic of such a multidimensional approach is that ethics, according to this view, is considered a key principle of good governance. It is also influenced by the characteristics and interaction of the political and legal context, as well as by economic policy[44]. Any effective ethics infrastructure should at the same time aim to control, guide and manage (also through better leadership) civil servants[45]. Consequently, it is an illusion to think that one instrument or one approach alone is sufficient to create an honest civil service with motivated and ethical civil servants.

Therefore, this study is based to a large extent on the hypothesis that an effective fight against wrongdoings requires a combination of holistic and detailed approaches. To this must be added the need to design effective instruments which fit into the national administrative culture and tradition. This means, for instance, that it is much more difficult to promote integrity in low trust countries than in high trust countries. Thus, even if discussions about ethics are relatively stable, ethical considerations always reflect the given social, cultural, political and economic context and the change of values in our societies.

Furthermore, various instruments must be in place to deal with different forms of misbehaviour. It seems evident that changing behaviour - such as reporting sick when not ill, showing minimal effort and commitment or the use of working hours for private purposes - which can clearly be identified as unethical, may require different instruments than it is the case for accepting a bribe in exchange for doing someone a favour. The first set of behaviours might be the result of demotivation or bad leadership, while the second may stem from the lack of monitoring capacities. In other cases, e.g. when officials are paid illegally for making certain decisions, it might even be difficult to find any effective instruments, as it might be impossible to prove the act even with increased monitoring.

---

44 For example, see World Bank, Anticorruption in transition: A contribution to the policy debate, Washington, 2000; OECD, Trust in government, op. cit.; OECD, Managing government ethics, Puma Policy Brief No. 1, Paris 1997.

45 OECD, Building public trust: Ethics measures in OECD countries, Puma Policy Brief No.7, Spring 2000.

Ethics is a complex issue and, as such, there must be many alternative patterns of causality that explain individual behaviour and individual fairness perceptions. Similarly, we acknowledge that the data collected stems from a too low sample, since only governmental representatives answered to this study. Answers were given by ethics and HRM experts from the responsible national ministries in the Member States of the EU. We were aware of the danger that some responses could be, to a certain degree, political biased, and tended to represent the official government's and/or the employer's point of view. One should also add that the collected data comes from a fairly homogenous group of experts from the same organisational level, prime ministers offices, central ministries or central agencies. Future research should include a much larger sample and it ought to cover lower level employees, top level civil servants, trade unions and employee representatives.

Other limitations include the methodology applied. All data in this study were collected through questionnaires, discussions and validations during two workshops and one top-level meeting under the Polish EU Presidency. We also invited some national delegations to present interesting case studies and good practices. The Dutch BIOS, the Latvian KNAB and the OECD took part in the EUPAN HR working group meeting and provided valuable information and insight.

Many discussions about the effectiveness of ethics have so far proven quite unsatisfactory. Almost no statistics, publications and facts exist on this subject. This is surprising since some Member States have established advanced and professional integrity systems, such as the Dutch Bureau Integriteitsbevordering Openbare Sector (BIOS), the British Committee on Standards in Public Life or The Corruption Prevention and Combating Bureau (KNAB) as well as sophisticated ethics infrastructures[46]. However, as already mentioned, only few studies have been carried out on the effectiveness of ethics systems and issues related to organisational justice (e.g., the impact of HR reforms on fairness perceptions and workplace behaviour).

---

46 See OECD, Trust in government: Ethics measures in OECD countries, Paris 2000.

3. DEFINING PUBLIC-SERVICE ETHICS IN ITS CONTEXT

3.1 Virtues and principles

Can there be too much or too little public ethics and public moral? According to Plato, there was no doubt that one of the most important tasks of the State was to educate its citizens to be moral and good citizens. For example, Plato supported the adoption of laws that obliged people to get married between 30 and 35 years. This is moral politics. Later on, Immanuel Kant argued that morality and law should be distinguished and separated from each other. Kant was very critical as to the role of the state in moral issues. According to Kant, the role of the state is not to educate its citizens in moral questions. The development of virtues is not a public task. Until today, this Kantian separation between moral and law is widely accepted. On the other hand, a certain tendency to revive moral politics can also be recognized.

Unfortunately, it is very difficult to adopt a clear criteria between the obligation of the state to interfere in moral issues and the need to abstain from moral politics. Do we live a revival of moral politics, for example as regards the introduction of public policies in the field of environmental awareness, health policies, anti-discrimination, anti-smoking and work ethos (performance and merit as guiding rules etc)? Or, is the state withdrawing from the discourse about moral and ethics? Or, both? Is the State becoming more influential in discussions around moral and ethics but, at the same time, citizens are becoming increasingly critical as to top-down induced values, rules and polices?

In fact, ethics is everywhere. The importance of ethics can not only be seen in the broader context of higher public expectations regarding quality of public services and credibility of public employees. Instead new discussions about corporate social responsibility of internationally operating companies, salaries of top managers, medical benefit of genetic engineering, euthanasia, ethics of green shareholding, social and cultural impact of the new media, our responsibility for climate change, healthy food requirements, anti-smoking policies, transparency and accountability requirement etc. reflect the ongoing importance of values and principles. In the field of public service ethics, "achieving an ethos of honesty and transparency becomes the Holy Grail"[47].

---

47 Oonagh Gay, Comparing systems of ethics regulation. In: Denis Saint-Martin/Fred Thompson (Eds.), Public ethics and governance: Standards and practices in comparative perspective. Vol. 14. Amsterdam/Boston/Heidelberg//New York/Oxford/Paris/San Diego/San Francisco/Singapore/Sydney/Tokyo, 2006, p. 107.

Today, almost no public organisation functions without constitutional principles and ethics codes that enumerate a number of virtues and principles which public officials should follow. The concepts of good governance and ethics rest on the assumption that it is possible to define what good administration and what ethical behaviour are. This requires a discussion about values and principles and about what should be achieved, and why? As regards the latter, the concept of ethics and ethical behaviour is still very much influenced by Aristotle´s distinction between virtues and vices. According to Aristotle, virtues and vices are contrary forms of human attitudes. Virtues are positive and vices are negative aspects of human behaviour. A virtue is a behaviour showing a high moral standard, and is a pattern of thought and behaviour based on high moral standards. Also for Aristotle, defining virtues was not an easy task. In his Nicomachean Ethics, Aristotle defined a virtue as a balance point between a deficiency and an excess of a trait. For example, courage is the mean between cowardice and foolhardiness, while tolerance is the mean between narrow-mindedness and over-acceptance. Vices are the opposites of virtues.

Later on, philosopher Kant doubted whether simple distinctions between good virtues and bad vices make sense. According to Kant, most virtues, as well as vices, are highly ambivalent and should always be judged in a specific context and whether (or not) they would serve a moral principle. In his Metaphysic of Morals Kant went even further: "Nothing can possibly be conceived in the world or even out of it, which can be called good, without qualification, except a good will"[48]. Right behavior requires acting for the right reason.

Luhmann wonders why moral and ethical behavior is still interpreted as either being moral (good) or immoral (bad, or even evil)[49]. In reality, ethical judgment is increasingly difficult since the trend towards more complex societies and the increased differentiation of state, government and society also make ethical judgments more difficult and complex[50]. Think about the need for ecological behaviour and sustainable consumption. More people find it important to live ethically but find it difficult to define limits for their actions ("am I am allowed to fly?", "is it ethical if I buy a bigger car?", "should I buy only regional products"?).

The increase in complexity in the society correlates with the increase in complexity of moral and ethics as such[51]. Moreover, the different societal systems

48 Immanuel Kant, Metaphysic of morals, in: Britannica Great Books, Vol. 42, p. 256.
49 Niklas Luhmann, Die Moral der Gesellschaft, Suhrkamp, Frankfurt/M., 2008, p. 115.
50 Ibid., p. 136.
51 Ibid., p. 156.

(the political system, public administration, the economical system, the legal system, science, religion etc.) function on the basis of different values[52]. Therefore, no country and no society are based on a uniform understanding of values and moral.

Still, today, more experts rediscover the importance of virtue-based ethics and are inspired by Aristotle´s famous formulation in the Nicomachean Ethics:"Neither by nature, then, nor contrary to nature do the virtues arise in us; rather we are adapted by nature to receive them, and are made perfect by habit (…). For the things we have to learn before we can do them, we learn by doing them…"[53]. Therefore, learning virtues can be difficult at first, but it becomes easier with practice over time until it becomes a habit.

Today, the Kantian as well as Aristotelean approaches are only partially applied. Instead, politicians and public managers typically approach ethics from the utilitarian perspective. They try to make ethical decisions that benefit the greatest number of employees or voters, and sometimes use bad means to achieve good ends. As Mearsheimer demonstrates, lying is used ever since as an instrument in international relations[54]. Despite this, it is widely recognized that we must seek moral and ethical limits on the use of these means. For this we need principles and virtues. In fact, we find plenty of ethical principles and values in our constitutions, laws and codes. In the meantime, administrations cannot afford the risk of functioning without an ethics code. At the same time, it seems, the Western societies have become so used to the existence of many ethical values and principles that we do not discuss their importance sufficiently, and, as a consequence, we are not cognisant about their exact meaning and how they relate to each other.

Despite all the differences that exist, all Member States agree that traditional principles (principle of impartiality, principle of legality, etc.) and specific ethics rules and standards are necessary for civil servants. The need for specific principles and rules is justified in all EU countries (the specific tasks of civil servants should be accompanied by specific duties and obligations). The most important principles in all Member States are the duty to respect the rule of law and to serve the common good (and the principle of democracy). Civil servants shall fulfil their tasks in an impartial and fair manner, and take into consideration the common interest. For example, Art. 153 of the Polish Constitution requires that

---

52 Ibid., p. 167.
53 Aristotle, Nicomachean Ethics, in: Britanica Great Books, Vol.9, p. 348.
54 John J. Mearsheimer, Why leaders lie: The truth about lying in international politics, Oxford University Press, New York, 2011.

"in order to ensure a professional, reliable, impartial and politically neutral discharge of the state's obligations, a corps of civil service shall operate in the organs of government administration". Other European-wide principles concern acceptance of gifts, the duty to take an oath, duties to treat certain issues as confidential or secret, duties to declare income, assets etc. Slightly different is the British example of the Seven Principles of Public Life[55], which is applicable to all Holders of Public Office and includes a number of very broad principles, such as selflessness, integrity, and objectivity (for more details see p. 130).

Consequently, the duties and obligations of civil servants often vary from and are much stricter than those of private sector employees. Still, all national civil service laws contain a number of detailed and specific duties and obligations for civil servants and also of employers. One good example is the Civil Servants Act in Slovenia which regulates a number of important principles such as the principle of equal access (Article 7), the principle of legality (in Article 8), the principle of professional conduct (Article 9), the principle of honourable conduct (Art. 10), the principle on the restriction and duties in respect of the acceptance of gifts (Art. 11), and the principle of confidentiality (Art. 12).

In some Member States specific obligations are even laid down in their respective Constitutions, or, may be otherwise directly derived from them. Article 103, clause III of the Spanish Constitution, for example, cites the safeguarding of the impartiality of civil servants in exercising their functions; according to Article 98 of the Italian Constitution, civil servants only serve the nation; and Article 269, clause I of the Portuguese Constitution commits civil servants to ensuring the common good. In Germany the obligation of neutrality is one of the central principles on which the civil service is founded and is constitutionally enshrined in Article 33, clause IV of the German Constitution. An indirect expression of the obligation of neutrality is given in Article 103, clause I of the Greek Constitution, according to which civil servants are to execute the will of the state and to serve the people. In Luxembourg, the duty of civil servants to observe neutrality can be indirectly derived from the oath, which Article 110 requires they swear.

The general obligation to perform tasks in a neutral fashion is expressed in concrete form in the various individual duties of the official. The neutrality of the public servant is safeguarded on the one hand, against financial influence, and against political influence on the other. Measures relating to the former include bans on the taking of bribes and the acceptance of gifts. More and more rules and regulations are also increasing in the field of conflicts of interests, post-

---

55 http://www.public-standards.gov.uk, last time checked on 26.3.2012.

employment, ancillary activities, multiple employments, etc. Overall, in the field of ethics, Holders of Public Office and civil servants are regulated much more strictly than other public and private sector employees. The focus in most Member States, however, is not only on the neutrality of the public employee with respect to financial influence, but also with respect to political influence – the aim being to safeguard the stability of the administration and provide a shield to the political forces that shape the life of the state.

In most EU Member States there is furthermore a duty of good faith or loyalty on the part of an employee of the civil service towards their employer; however, the importance of this duty varies among the different Member States. This is particularly true with regard to loyalty to the constitution, which is more far-reaching in Germany than anywhere else. In contrast, the duty of obedience with respect to official instructions was for a long time incumbent on public employees in all EU Member States, and essentially served to highlight their subordination to instructions. How far that subordination extends today, however, is not clear in all Member States. In some, the threshold is the point at which a public employee is instructed to commit a punishable offence.

Other additional rules with regard to duties and obligations differ from country to country. For example, in the German Civil Service Law, 26 paragraphs deal with specific rights and obligations. These range from notifications to the media ("the Director of the institution decides who should provide information to the media"), the acceptance of gifts, specific references relating to clothing, the choice of an apartment (which should be not too far away from the place of work), the duty to take an oath and many other issues. Many of these duties and obligations do not exist in other Member States. For example, paragraph 78 regarding the Fürsorgepflicht des Dienstherrn (duty of the employer or superior to take care of the civil servant). This paragraph obliges the superior/employer to take care of the civil servant and his family even after the end of their career in the civil service. According to this philosophy, the civil servant is not an ordinary state employee, but remains a civil servant – for their whole life. Consequently, it is expected that a civil servant is acting faithfully to the state and – in exchange – the State takes care of the civil servant.

As the answers to this study show, many traditional (bureaucratic) principles, standards and ethical obligations are still in place. Moreover, traditional principles like the German *Fuersorgepflicht* or *Alimentationsprinzip* have never been changed. This is remarkable given the enormous changes that have taken place in other areas during the last years. In fact, the present reform trends towards post-bureaucratic structure have led to the adoption of more codes that govern the behaviour of civil servants. Thus, despite all ongoing reform trends in the past and efforts to deregulate HRM policies, specific rules concerning duties and obligations have become more numerous in the field. Instead, it is a field of re-regulation and mostly in the field of codes, conflicts of interests, anti-discrimination, diversity, accountability, performance management, transparency and citizen-orientation.

Strangely enough, discussions about the need for (new) values and value management have become more important than discussions about how principles and values can be applied in practice. For example, applying the principle of impartiality can be a difficult undertaking as the principle as such is very broad and can be interpreted in many different ways[56]. The same concerns the implementation of the principle of equity (e.g. through the implementation of merit based approaches) and the principle of equality (e.g. through the implementation of standardised approaches and the principle of non-discrimination). In daily HR policies, the application of both principles may create dilemmas and contradictions – and unintentional effects.

In reality, combining and respecting all principles and values at the same time can be a difficult task. According to Briggs, "the overemphasis on one value or group of values can have the effect of undermining others. No value should be pursued to the point of direct conflict with another"[57]. For example, the principle of loyalty can conflict with the principle of legality and the principle of impartiality.

In this study, we take a middle approach. Firstly, we claim that ethical behaviour can be learned and cultivated. Secondly, we believe that values and virtues as such are ambivalent and sometimes even contradictory concepts. In some cases, even positive values can have very ambivalent effects. Moreover, the discussion on what constitutes the cardinal virtues is changing over time. For example, virtues such as modesty or impartiality must always be interpreted in the context and time. In the same way, it becomes more difficult to define vices and unethical behaviour in times of changing governance and changing values. According to the philosopher Seel[58], only cruelty is clearly negative. All other vices are also ambivalent concepts.

---

56 Susan Mendus, Impartiality, in: John S. Dryzek/Bonnie Honig/Anne Philips (Eds.), The Oxford Handbook of Political Theory, Oxford University Press, New York, 2006, pp. 423-435.

57 Briggs, Testing APS ethics, op. cit., p. 119.

58 Martin Seel, 111 Tugenden, 111 Laster, Fischer, Frankfurt/Main, 2011.

Thirdly, working ethically and under the guidance of a number of virtues is not more nor less challenging than leading an ethically correct private life. Buying ethically, investing ethically, eating and drinking ethically, travelling ethically, driving ethically, raising your children ethically... In "*A life stripped bare. My year trying to live ethically*", the journalist of the British Guardian, Leo Hickman tries. His novel is a breath-taking illustration of how difficult, if not impossible, it is to live ethically. "It is easier to teach, preach, study, advocate, debate and publish ethics than to practice ethical living"[59].

3.2 Public values and public ethics

As we have seen in the previous subchapter, public services need guidance through values and principles. But how do values and principles change and develop? And how does this impact on the effectiveness of ethics? When looking back, it seems that since Aristotle's Nichomachean Ethics every "era (…) has a few words that epitomize its world-view and that are fixed points by which all else can be measured. During the antic times these were virtues such as Justice and Courage; in the Middle Ages they were religious values such words as faith, grace, and God; in the eighteenth century they were such rational concepts and words such as reason, nature, and rights..."[60]. Today, these words seem to be complex concepts such as efficiency, merit, accountability, flexibility and good governance.

Also public service values such as neutrality, stability, hierarchy, confidentiality, loyalty and impartiality, have a different meaning nowadays than before[61]. In fact, values do not perish - they change. Thus, there has never been a static concept and a uniform understanding of public values and public ethics. Moreover, it is difficult to show whether values get lost.

Today, people are becoming more demanding and critical as to leaders and authorities, but also more critical towards their own life aspirations. At the same time, there are more uncertainties about the existence of universal values and the nature of values. One may even say that where the state, politicians and other political, administrative and religious leaders are perceived more critically than ever before, citizens continue to apply higher standards to themselves and their

---

59 Leo Hickman, A life stripped bare. My year trying to live ethically, Eden, 2006.

60 Dwight Waldo, The administrative state, Ronald Press, New York, 1948, p. 19.

61 Zeger van der Wal, Value solidity, differences, similarities and conflicts between the organisational values of government and business, Dissertation at the Free University of Amsterdam, 2008.

conceptions of religion, belief, luck and self-fulfilment. Never before have people been so demanding as to their own self-fulfilment and self-development.

As Schulze[62] shows we experience a decade of moral relativism and moral tolerance but not an age of moral decline. Even to the contrary: this rise of expectations in the field of ethics is to be welcomed since it reflects that citizens' attitudes towards authorities have become more critical and more mature. Today, citizens display less tolerance to unethical behaviour than ever before.

Still, many observers fear a loss of values as a consequence of the present moral relativism[63]. One should bear in mind that the latter is as old as mankind. For example, the well-known French sociologist Emile Durkheim introduced his concept of anomie in 1893[64].He used anomie to describe a condition that was occurring in society, i.e. that the rules on how people ought to behave towards each another were breaking down. Anomie, simply defined, is a state where norms are confused, unclear or absent. According to Durkheim, it is a situation of normlessness. Anomie, therefore, refers to a breakdown of social norms and it is a condition where norms no longer control the activities of society members. Changing conditions as well as adjustment of life leads to dissatisfaction, conflict, and deviance. Durkheim observed that social periods of disruption, e.g. economic depression, brought about greater *anomie*. Durkheim felt that sudden societal change caused a state of anomie. A similar theory was presented later on in the USA by Robert Merton[65]. However, both authors did not explain why new values and norms are developing, too.

Cooper argues that "we are in a time of transition in which the modern heritage of public administration is increasingly in conflict with a postmodern model"[66]. The key phenomena of modernity are assumptions about universal values, absolute values, bureaucracy and rationality. Contrary to this, postmodern is a term in which "fundamental assumptions are being discredited as final and absolute. Assumptions about some kind of objectively real and universal human nature, or natural law, or absolute values and ultimate truths (...) no longer hold..."[67]. "The homogeneity of traditional society, with its unifying and stabilising cultural bonds, has been broken (...). New forms of lifestyles have developed, and new

---

62 Gerhard Schulze, Die Sünde, Carl Hanser, München, 2006.
63 Steven Lukes, Moral relativism, Picador, New York, 2008.
64 Emile Durkheim, The division of labour in society, Free Press, 1997.
65 Robert K. Merton, Social structure and anomie, in: American Sociological Review, Vol. 3, No. 5/1938, pp. 672-682.
66 Terry L. Cooper, The responsible administrator, Jossey Bass, 5th edition, 2006, p. 45.
67 Ibid., p. 46.

ways of coping with a broad spectrum of lifestyles, diets, preferences, political philosophies, and modes of exchange have evolved"[68]. The implications of these changes for public administration are obvious: post-modern administrations tend to be much more diverse, less hierarchical, more flexible, diverse, representative and less separated from the citizenry. Whereas the term bureaucracy represents clear values, such as hierarchy, formalism, standardisation, rationality and obedience, the term postmodernism implies conflicting values and value dilemmas.

The problem with this description of the administration in the 21st century is obvious. Whereas the term "bureaucracy" or "modernity" can be defined and broken down into concrete contents, this is much less the case with the term "postmodernity". The latter represents a fluid notion and neither offers a clear definition nor orientation. Although the term postmodernism may be an adequate description of the current change processes, it leaves those in charge of introducing change processes puzzled. The notion postmodern administration illustrates that we lack an understanding of what could be an (universal) alternative to the bureaucratic form of organisation. Mostly the terms postmodern, post-bureaucratic organisation or post-public service are nothing but negative "counter" definitions.

Today, the current trend towards a postmodern public service reminds us about the importance of values and principles. Bourdieu, Coleman and mostly Putnam have showed that shared values and trust are important components of social capital. Putnam has defined social capital as "features of social organisation, such as trust, norms, and networks, that can improve the efficiency of society by facilitating coordinated actions"[69] Putnams central theme was that people have chosen steadily to withdraw from civil life. As a result this individualisation trend destroys social capital and the social cohesion of the society. Similarly to Putnam, but less focused on political science approaches, Ehrenberg shows in the field of psychology that societal trends towards ever more individualisation and autonomy support the emergence of new psychological disorders (e.g. the increasing numbers of depressions and burn outs)[70]. Still, it is difficult to analyse whether social capital is threatened and whether this has effects on the ethical behaviour of people.

In 2003, two studies were published in the Netherlands on the development of values and norms in the Dutch society (including some comparative observa-

---

68 Ibid., p. 52.
69 R. D. Putnam, Making democracy work: Civil traditions in modern Italy, Princeton, 1993, p.169.
70 Alain Ehrenberg, La societe du malaise, Odile Jacob, 2010.

tions with respect to various European countries)[71]. A report by the Dutch Scientific Council for Governmental Policy (Wetenschappelijke Raad voor het Regeringsbeleid – WRR)) and a report on norms and values (Waarden, Normen en de last van het gedrag)[72]. However, the results of both reports, as well as of another survey about "Moral in the public opinion" (2004) contrasted to some degree with the popular stereotypes regarding an on-going moral and ethical decline in our societies. In fact, both studies concluded that citizens have surprisingly clear attitudes about what they believe is accepted as moral and ethical behaviour and what is not. Regarding the question whether existing laws must be respected and enforced, for example, only a very small minority believed that this should not be the case.

Also, the acceptance of the rule of law, individual freedoms, e.g. the right to express an opinion, right to be protected against discrimination, right to vote, support for the principle of democracy, etc. are still very widely accepted among European citizens. In addition, voluntary engagement in religious, political or cultural organisations is not decreasing but remains quite stable. Furthermore, the growing individualism in our societies does not seem to lead to less voluntary social engagement. "Individualism is not the same as egoism"[73].

Still, in today´s discussions on public values, it is all too often assumed that one universal set of values exists[74], whereas recent research shows that values differ according to different organisations[75]. Consequently, some authors discuss the need to safeguard public values against private sector values. Hence, artificial distinctions between public and private values are upheld. In fact, de Graaf and van de Wal show that that "the values of profitability, competitiveness, and cus-

---

71 Paul Dekker/Joep de Hart/Paul de Beer/Christa Hubers, De moraal in de publieke opinie (Morals in Public Opinion), Social and Cultural Planning Agency [Sociaal en Cultureel Planbureau], The Hague, 2004, http://www.scp.nl, last time checked on 26.3.2012; Wetenschappelijke Raad voor het Regeringsbeleid WRR (Scientific Council for Government Policy), Waarden, normen en de last van het gedrag (Values, standards and the burden of behaviour), The Hague, 2003.

72 Wetenschappelijke Raad voor het Regeringsbeleid WRR, Waardenn Normen en de last van het gedrag, op. cit.

73 Paul Dekker/Joep de Hart/Paul de Beer/Christa Hubers, De moraal in de publieke opinie, op. cit., p. 81.

74 Zeger van der Wal/E. Th. van Hout (2009), Is public value pluralism paramount? The intrinsic multiplicity and hybridity of public values, in: International Journal of Public Administration, Vol. 32, 3-4/2009, pp. 220-231.

75 Sandra van Thiel/Zeger van der Wal, Birds of a feather? The effect of organisational value congruence on the relationship between ministries and quangos, in: Public Organisation Review, Vol. 10 No 4/2010, pp. 377-397.

tomer orientation have a greater influence on business decisions; in public organisations, values such as legitimacy, lawfulness, accountability, and impartiality play a larger role. However, great differences exist among the organisations within each sector"[76].

In the meantime, new values such as transparency, diversity, sustainability and flexibility have also been added to the classical values. As it seems, the future will be dominated by more value conflicts and newly emerging values. For example, over the past ten years, "the number of countries identifying transparency as a core public service value almost doubled"[77]. Also, efficiency is seen as an increasingly important value. Thus, it may well be that in ten years' time privacy, or alternatively risk protection, may become ever more important values. Moreover, some ethical problems may be resolved and others will emerge. Therefore, dilemma training for civil servants may become more important than in the past.

Figure 2. Frequently stated public service core values (2000 and 2009)[78]

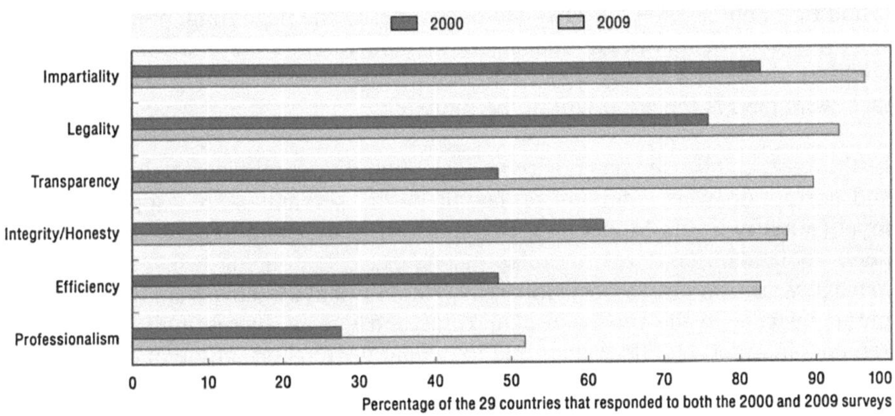

The change of values also merits the discussion of another question: what are the effects of the growing importance of individual values, such as significance of individual performance. Today, public employees want to be seen as individuals and be treated individually according to their personal performance levels. Consequently, traditional pay systems with their career ladders, time-based

76 Gjalf de Graaf/Zeger van der Wal, On value differences experienced by sector switchers, in: Administration and Society, Vol. 40, No.1/ 2008, p.79.

77 Ibid.

78 OECD, Governance at a glance, Paris, 2009, p. 40.

pay increases and specific allowances, reflect a slowly disappearing concept of employment. Today, employees themselves expect immediate rewards and recognition for their individual accomplishments e.g. if two employees perform similar jobs, but one has a greater workload, he/she wants a better pay. This individualisation process is further enhanced through the introduction of individual accountability mechanisms and the introduction of sophisticated performance measurement and performance management techniques. The introduction of these techniques may favour individual performance orientation instead of corporate thinking for the common good. However, very little is known about the change of fairness conceptions, values and their impact on ethical behaviour in the national public services.

3.3 Public-service ethics and public ethos – different than business ethics?

As we have seen in the previous chapters, neither virtues, values nor the public service ethos were ever a static and homogenous concept. Their meaning has developed and changed continuously from the past to the present. Also the definition of a civil servant has changed over time. In the beginning, public servants were servants of the kings, queens, Lords and Royals; they had no rights and could be dismissed at any time. Although most of them belonged to the elite, they were paid at the good will of the monarch.

In the past, public servant positions were bought, acquired or sold. Nepotism and corruption were common, although public servants were supposed to be loyal (initially to the Monarchs), to pledge allegiance and to obey the royal orders. Their main task was to collect taxes, exercise policing tasks, prepare and manage wars and protect the Monarchy. Recruitment systems were not based on merit: instead, in the medieval age, kings and queens increasingly "recruited" servants in order to collect taxes and to defend the territory of the monarchy. For the first time, this practice became a routine under the reign of Philippe le Bel (1285-1314) who systematically concentrated on the recruitment of lawyers specialised in Roman law[79].

This historical role of civil servants as dependent instruments of the monarchy explains why later civil service concepts focused so much on rules, procedures and rationality. In fact, the objective was to make civil servants independent from particular and personal interests. In Europe the emergence of independent and impartial civil services is closely linked to the emergence of the Republican

79 http://www.vie-publique.fr/decouverte-institutions/institutions/approfondissements/histoire-fonction-publique.html, last time checked on 26.3.2012.

State (firstly in France) and the Nation State (especially after the Congress of Vienna in 1815)[80]. In France, the public law status was invented during the French Revolution in order to link the civil servants to the State and not to the Monarchy[81].

However, the realisation of an independent civil service was more difficult than expected. At the end of the 18th century and until the 19th century, the absolute right of the employer to discharge a worker coincided with the sovereignty doctrine in the public sector. Because employment was a privilege, not a right, it was subject to terms specified by government. "Government is sovereign; it is inappropriate to dilute its management rights (...). Indeed for much of the nineteenth century (...) the spoils system dominated personnel policy. (...) Public office was perverted into a private fiefdom as arrogance, greed, and opportunism prevailed over honour, openness and prudence. Favouritism, cronyism, intimidation, corruption, waste, scandals and rampant dismissals were widespread in that squalid era. Rather than governance; its highest priority was to reward its friends, to grant favours for favours given."[82]

This practice changed slowly. Bekke and van der Meer[83] define civil service systems as depersonalised systems which differ from traditional modes of government. The biggest changes included the introduction of merit principles such as entrance examinations, job tenure, career service, and political neutrality, which were adopted as a moral guardian to democracy and which should shield employees from politically inspired employment actions. "In all cases, and particularly in Britain, France, Prussia and Spain, the emergence of a central state in combination with the centralisation of authority is considered an important explanatory factor in the growing reliance of rulers on both military and civilian officials. The multiplication of government tasks and the increasing level of administrative specialisation eventually made the separation of the personal and the administrative household of the ruler inevitable (...). It was initially an or-

---

80 Hagen Schulze, Staat und Nation in der europäischen Geschichte, Beck, 2004, p. 39.

81 "Le premier souci des républicains, dès la fin des années 1870, est de s'assurer des sentiments favorables des fonctionnaires à l'égard de la République: la fonction publique", http://diffusion.vie-publique.fr/decouverte-institutions/institutions/ apprfondissements/histoire-fonction-publique.html, last time checked on 26.3.2012.

82 James S. Bowman/Jonathan P. West, Removing employee protection: A "see no evil" approach to civil service reform, in: Leo W. J. Huberts/Jeroen Maesschalck/Carole Jurkiewicz, Ethics and integrity of governance: Perspectives across frontiers, Edward Elgar, Massachusetts, 2008, p. 183.

83 Hans A.G. M. Bekke/Frits M. van der Meer, Civil service systems in Western Europe, Edward Elgar Publishing Ltd, 2000.

ganisational division, but it also symbolised a profound change in authority relationships. These changing roles represent an important institutionalised shift, as the authority relations of civil servants towards the ruler (gradually) became less personalised (...). Civil servants gradually evolved from personal servants in the service of the ruler to servants of the state"[84].

Many changes on the continent were actually realised as a consequence of the Napoleonic wars and conquests. "Politico-administrative renewal was either imported or renewed..."[85] (...) "Instrumental in effectuating these changes was the establishment of the Rechtsstaat or in Anglo-Saxon terms the rule of law (...) This powerful idea had implications for the relation between government and the civil service system. (...) Step by step the legal position of civil servants in all countries was formalised and standardised. (...) Merit instead of privilege was becoming the guiding principle"[86]. The status of the civil servants evolved into a protected status with many specific employment features that differed from ordinary employment patterns.

As such, the creation of a modern civil service is a response to the emergence of the liberal state which was based on the rule of law. Despite this common frame, many civil service systems differed and had too specific reform trajectories. At the same time, criticism emerged in relation to the (often perceived as inflexible) protected nature of the civil service. Consequently, civil service criticism is strongly linked with the emergence of a specific civil service. "Bureaucratic bashing" is at least two hundred years old.

Ironically, one of the first modern European civil services was not set up in Europe, but rather in India by the East India Company, distinguishing its civil servants from its military servants[87]. As early as 1793, the British government developed a civil service code for the territory of India "under which officials received reasonable if not lavish pay and conditions of service. The important question of promotion was regularised in accordance with the rule of seniority as laid down in the Charter Act of 1793. It was regarded as a safeguard against favouritism and unfairness…".[88] In order to prevent corruption and favouritism, promotions within the company were based on examinations. The system then

---

84 Ibid., p. 276.

85 Ibid., p. 277.

86 Ibid., p. 278.

87 Edgar Norman Gladden, Civil services of the United Kingdom 1856-1970, Frank Cass, London, 1967.

88 Edgar Norman Gladden, A history of public administration, Vol. II, Frank Cass, London, 1972, p. 251.

spread to the United Kingdom in 1854 (based on in the Northcote-Trevelyan report which was published more than 150 years ago)[89].

Lifetime tenure was first introduced in Bavaria in Germany in 1805[90]. Later on the so-called *Alimentationsprinzip* was established which obliged civil servants to devote their whole personality (and full working time) to the public employer. On the other hand, the public employer was obliged to take care of the civil servant (and his family) for their whole life (from here stems the request to have specific pension systems for civil servants). In Prussia, the "Allgemeines Landrecht für die Preußischen Staaten" of 1794 contained 19.000 paragraphs[91]. Elsewhere, different cities in Italy (and later in the State of Italy), different regions in Spain and parts of the Netherlands invented their own civil service models and further adapted them to regional and national tradition, culture and political needs. More and more, in all European societies it was believed that civil servants were linked to the authority of the state and could not be compared to other public employees or employees in the private sector.

At the beginning of the twentieth century, almost all Member States designed their public organisations as bureaucratic systems, for they expected that certain behaviours on the part of civil servants would result from specific organisational features. Traditionally, a hierarchical and formalised organisational structure, clear and rigid career paths, lifetime tenure, full-time employment, seniority, advantageous pension systems and rigid remuneration systems were introduced in order to reduce, as far as possible, the risk of too much political influence, corruption, misconduct, the exercise of private interests and instability of government. Consequently, the traditional argument for a specific organisational structure was to produce a certain ethical status for civil servants who should be committed to the public good, neutrality, impartiality and to observing confidentiality and displaying expertise. In many countries, civil servants were therefore working in hierarchical organisations, had very specific recruitment procedures, specific ethical obligations, little mobility, varying working conditions and specific social security systems. Since the notion of social services was in existence for a short time only[92], most existing "civil services" were tax services, military and judicial services and police services. Consequently, the most important task

---

89 Stafford Northcote/C. E. Trevelyan, The organisation of the permanent civil service, Parliamentary Papers, Volume XXVII, 1854.

90 Matthias Pechstein/Rudolf Summer, Beiträge zum Beamtenrecht, Tuebingen, 2007, p. 58.

91 Schulze, Staat und Nation in der europäischen Geschichte, op. cit., p. 96.

92 For instance, until the 1950s, only a few countries had anti-poverty programmes or initiatives in the field of food safety, social security or environmental protection.

of the state sector was to control society rather than to serve society. The Leviathan (T. Hobbes) stood above society and governments were – until the 1970s – more concerned with the implementation of programmes than with the evaluation of their outcomes. Moreover, citizens were not allowed to question government authorities at all.

Within this bureaucratic structure, where the public service was closed off and separated from society and citizens, it was not possible for civil servants to the have the right to strike or the right to engage in collective agreements relating to working conditions. In other words, civil servants were seen as a different category of staff. Because of the specific treatment of civil servants, public perceptions arose of civil servants having different personalities, being motivated by different incentives, working less hard than employees in the private sector, being more security-minded, more rule-oriented and not very innovative.

Still, it is important to remind that the emerging modern concept of bureaucracy and civil service was by nature a republican concept that was designed as a counter concept to the traditional and charismatic power structure of the monarchist and medieval times. As such, the bureaucracy as described by Weber was believed to be an impartial instrument of power which was based on the principle of rationality. Its task was to enhance the stability of the state while limiting the influence of the (political) class. Yet, bureaucracy was not only supposed to be a new form of rational power, it was also believed to be more efficient and more ethical than any other organisational form. The real turning point was the Holocaust, which demonstrated the perverse effects of instrumental bureaucratic rationality.[93]

Most of the new Member States who joined European Union in 2005 opted for structures with classical career paths. One major reason for establishing a career system was to combat the problem of political influence and patronage stemming from the Communist period. Consequently, civil servants have different and often stricter duties and obligations than private sector employees. Still, all national civil service laws contain a number of detailed and specific duties and obligations for civil servants and also for the employers. Despite all the differences that exist, also the old EU Member States agree that traditional principles

---

93 For example, T. W. Adorno/E. Frenkel-Brunswik/D. J. Levinson/R.N. Sanford, The authoritarian personality, New York, Harper and Row, 1950; Stanley Milgram, Obedience to authority, Harper Perennial, 1983; Zygmunt Bauman, Dialektik der Ordnung – Die Moderne und der Holocaust, Europäische Verlagsanstalt, Hamburg, 2000; Philip Zimbardo, The Lucifer effect: Understanding how good people turn evil, Random House, 2008.

such as impartiality and legality, and specific ethics rules and standards are necessary for civil servants.

For example, Swedish civil servants are required to know a number of principles and understand their importance for the work in their agencies, and in their encounters with citizens and other parties. Officials must also be prepared for situations where these principles come into conflict with each other, and they must use good judgement in approaching these situations and taking action[94]. These principles include the following:

- Democracy - all public power in Sweden stems from the people, universal suffrage, representative democracy and parliamentary system;
- Legality - public power shall be exercised under the law;
- Objectivity, impartiality and equal treatment - equality of all persons before the law. Government agencies and courts must treat all persons equally;
- Free formation of opinions and freedom of expression - Swedish democracy is founded on the free formation of opinions;
- Respect - public power shall be exercised with respect for the freedom and equality of every person;
- Efficiency and service - public sector activities must be conducted as inexpensively and with as high quality as possible, given the resources available.

All of these principles are as modern as they are traditional. The most important principle in all Member States is the duty to respect the law and to serve the common good (and the principle of democracy), with the two being, at times, conflicting principles. Civil servants shall fulfil their tasks in an impartial and fair manner, and take into consideration the common interest. Other European-wide principles concern acceptance of gifts, the duty to take an oath, duties to treat certain issues as confidential or secret, duties to declare income, assets, etc. In most Member States of the EU, there is furthermore a duty of good faith or loyalty on the part of an employee of the civil service towards their employer. However, the importance of this principle varies among the different Member States. This is particularly true with regard to loyalty to the constitution.

As we have seen, many traditional bureaucratic principles, standards and ethical obligations are still in place. In fact, a number of traditional principles have never

---

94 Swedish Council for Strategic Human Resources Development, Shared values for civil servants, Stockholm, no year.

changed. Their purpose is to ensure an impartial public service which is based on the rule of law. Thus, the purpose of a public servant is to represent the public service ethos. This legitimacy has never lost its meaning. However, in the meantime, societal and individual values have changed. Today, values and principles clash. This changing process calls into question the traditional legitimacy of the public service ethos. Still, this process is full of ambivalences, as it is not clear how new values support an impartial and depoliticed republican public service.

However, a number of traditional principles have also shown contradictory effects. For example, too much centralisation, too little flexibility, not enough openness, responsibility and citizen orientation. As Demmke and Moilanen[95] have shown, countries with bureaucratic features are not necessarily less corrupt than post-bureaucratic systems (see Figure 3 on page 47). Even more, some Scandinavian post-bureaucratic systems show lower levels of corruption than certain classical bureaucratic states. "One could interpret as an argument that bureaucratic features as such are not necessary to ensure ethical government. In fact, this could be a strong argument against many classical bureaucratic principles. Institutional aspects alone are not sufficient for establishing a link between ethics, corruption and the civil service system"[96].

3.4 Public service motivation and public-service ethos

Despite all public management reforms, surprisingly little is still known about the relationship between organisational reform and individual behaviour. At the end of the 19th century Woodrow Wilson was the first to be become interested in the performance of civil servants and whether public service motivation would be specific as such. Not much later, Max Weber observed that there was a connection between organisational structure and personality. According to Weber, the individual becomes a cog in the machinery of modern bureaucracy. Despite the fact that he believed that no other organisational model was more efficient and powerful than private or public bureaucracies, he was also concerned about the impact of bureaucracies on the personality of those who worked in it.

---

95 Christoph Demmke/Timo Moilanen, Civil services in the EU of 27, Peter Lang, Frankfurt/M., 2010, p. 232-234.

96 Ibid., p. 233.

Figure 3. Relation between the traditional bureaucracy – post-bureaucracy continuum and the corruption perception index[97]

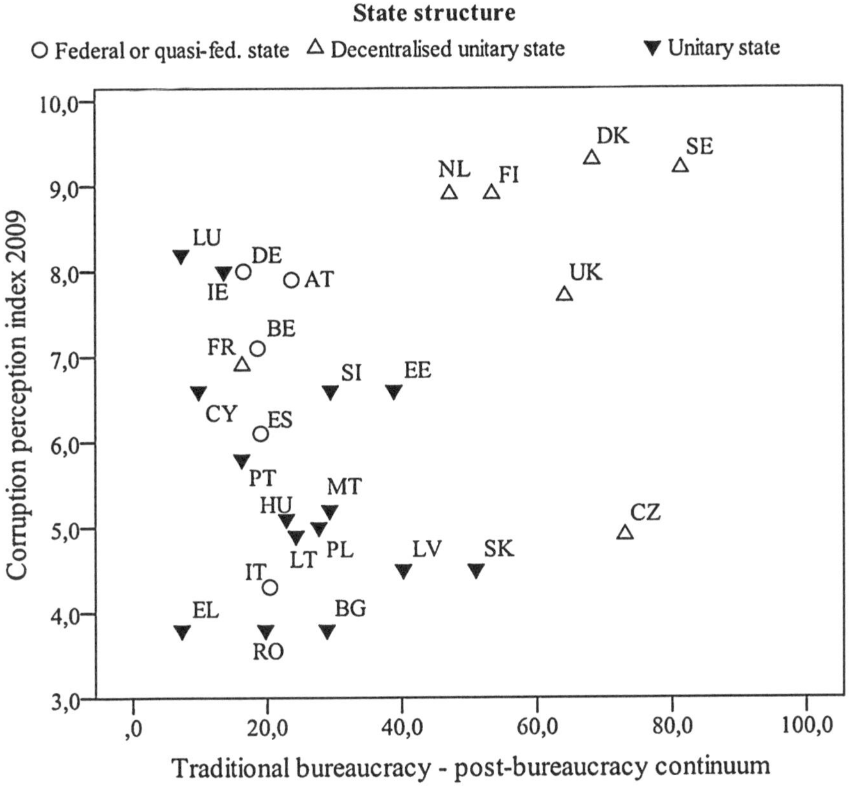

Max Weber would certainly have subscribed to the phrase of Winston Churchill's famous remark on democracy and turned it into "Bureaucracy is the worst form of organisation – except for all the rest". According to Bozeman, "We do not love bureaucracy, but we need it, at least until we devise workable alternative organisational schemes that permit us to retain the features of bureaucracy that we embrace eagerly – predictability and stability, rationality, reliance on expertise, equitable treatment – while discarding the features we hate – rigidity,

97 Christoph Demmke/Timo Moilanen, Civil services in the EU of 27, Peter Lang, Frankfurt/M., 2010, p. 233.

inability to deal with special needs, and a setting of barriers between officialdom and citizens."[98]

The American sociologist Merton[99] was actually the first scientist to analyse the connection between personality and bureaucratic structure. According to him "...the bureaucratic structure exerts a constant pressure upon the official to be methodical, prudent, disciplined. (...). An effective bureaucracy demands reliability of response and strict devotion to regulations...."[100]. Still, Merton's explanations supported the view of the entrepreneur as an innovator and individualist and the civil servant as a conformist and someone avoiding innovation. At the same time, the notion of a bureaucratic personality and the belief that adult personality socialisation develops through work organisation emerged. A widespread popular assumption suggests that specific public tasks, objectives (working for the common good), organisational structures (hierarchical and bureaucratic structures) and working conditions, e.g. life-time tenure, do cause changes and influence personality.

The above means that changing organisational structures, working conditions and value requirements in the public service will also influence the personality and the behaviour of a civil servant. Still, discussions focus on the nature of public sector motivation, but less on the development of ethical behaviour.
Against all "bureaucratic wisdom" Goodsell concluded that bureaucrats are ordinary people. They teach children, manage forests, program computers, chase speeders, arbitrate labour disputes, calculate benefit-cost ratios, inspect meat, enforce environmental permits, conduct research, negotiate contracts, prepare laws, fight wars, etc." Within a point or two, bureaucrats as a whole are identical with the general public in their concern about crime, drugs, the environment, welfare, and the condition of the cities. Their views are similar close on capital punishment, premarital sex, school bussing, and fundamentalist religion. Overall, comparability outweighs contrast..."[101]

---

98 Barry Bozeman, Bureaucracy and red tape, Prentice Hall, New Jersey, 2000. See especially the preface and page 19.

99 Robert K Merton, Bureaucratic structure and personality, in: Jay M Shafritz/ Albert C. Hyde, Classics of public administration, The Dorsey Press, Chicago, Illinois, 2. edition, 1987, p. 111.

100 Ibid., p. 112.

101 Ibid., p. 114.

On the other hand, Perry[102] developed a measurement scale which consists of four dimensions: attraction to policy making, commitment to the public interest and civic duty, compassion, and self-sacrifice. The findings suggested that people who are attracted to working in the public services have unique motivational incentives that energise and direct their behaviour. Consequently, the motivational aspects of work in the public service cannot be fully explained by rational and public choice theories. In fact, the different dimension of work in the public service shows that rational and egoistic motives are the only two explanatory variables for work in the public service[103].

Despite the fact that research in the field of public service motivation theory is expanding fast[104], its relative importance is unclear[105]. Still, many questions remain unanswered[106]. Far too little research has been carried out so far on comparative public service motivation. It is not yet clear as to whether and how motivation differs within the public service, civil service, between different governmental levels and different categories of staff. It is also unclear as to whether and how public service motivation differs from the core governmental level, to agencies, semi-public bodies to public private partnerships (and also into the private sector). So far the concept has been applied far too homogenously and does not reflect the growing differentiation within the public service. Moreover, international research is only about to start. The concept as such was for a long time dominated by US approaches[107]. However, it may well be that different

---

102 James Perry, Measuring public service motivation: An assessment of construct reliability and validity, in: Journal of Public Administration Research and Theory, Vol. 6, No. 1/1996. pp. 5-22.

103 Gerhard Hammerschmid/Renate E. Meyer/Isabel Egger-Peitler, Das Konzept der Public Service Motivation – Status Quo der internationalen Diskussion und erste empirische Evidenzen für den deutschsprachigen Raum, in: Der moderne Staat, Zeitschrift für Public Policy, Recht und Management Heft 1/2009, p. 73.

104 James Perry/Annic Hondeghem (Eds.), Motivation in public management, Oxford 2008.

105 Peter Leisink/Bram Steijn, Recruitment, attraction and selection, in: Perry/Hondeghem, Motivation in public management, op. cit., p. 124.

106 Yves Emery/Carole Wyser, Identities of public sector employees as a source of inspiration for differentiating HRM practices: The Swiss case. Paper presented at the EGPA Conference, 2-5 September 2009.

107 Pablo Alonso/Gregory Lewis, Public service motivation and job performance: Evidence from the federal sector, in: American Review of Public Administration, Vol. 31, No. 4/2001, pp. 363-380; Gene A. Brewer/Sally Colman Selden/Rex L. Facer II, Individual conceptions of public service motivation, in: Public Administration Review, Vol. 60, No. 3/2000, pp. 254-264; David Houston, Public service motivation: A multivariate test, in: Journal of Public Administration Research and Theory, Vol. 10, No. 4/2000, pp. 713-727.

administrative cultures and public service systems have a different influence on public service motivation.

Another question is how ethics management correlates with public service motivation[108] since a number of values are not included in the public service motivation concept (e.g., impartiality, integrity)[109]. Moreover, it is far from clear whether a strong public service motivation is something positive or whether it may also contribute to unethical conduct[110]. Although they have a lot in common, public motivation theories should not be mixed with public ethics theories. Both theories point to the likelihood of different values and motives in the public services. However, having different motivational motives than in the private sector does not mean that public servants are better employees or that they act more ethically[111].

3.5 The change of workplace ethics and values

Values are often interchanged with ethics. While there is a close and often interdependent relationship between the two, such interchanging is problematic[112]. Ethics is about determining what is right, wrong or bad, and these ethical choices and decisions are informed by values. Today, public-service ethics is influenced by a greater number and variety of conflicting values. Finally, one could also say that, whereas classical public-service ethics is relatively conservative and has endured over time, public service reforms are requiring public officials to respect new and more values.

Take the case of work ethics. A century ago, Max Weber[113] described a tendency within Protestant, capitalist societies for rich and poor alike to work for the sake of work. Under the Protestant work ethic, Weber explained, the highest good is to combine the earning of more and more money with the "strict avoidance of all spontaneous enjoyment in life". Instead of working to live, the Protestants lived to work. Consequently, work was the context for the display of moral and practical virtues. Pay systems were based on the principle of procedural fairness, the principle of standardisation and seniority. They were not de-

---

108 Jeroen Maesschalck/Zeger van der Wal/Leo Huberts, Public service motivation and ethical conduct, in: Perry/Hondeghem, Motivation in public management, op. cit., pp. 157-177.

109 Ibid., pp. 161-162.

110 Ibid.

111 Ibid., p. 171.

112 Ibid.

113 Max Weber, The protestant ethic and the spirit of capitalism, Penguin Books, 2002.

signed as a direct payment for individual work done, but compensation for their service as a whole, in other words, for civil servants making their entire working capacity available to the general public and carrying out their duties to the best of their ability. Today, most pay systems are based on the principle of individual performance and distributional fairness. The new pay systems are flexible and designed as a direct payment for individual work done. However, this does not suggest that flexible and performance related pay systems are fairer than traditional systems. Instead, they are based on a different understanding of fairness and reflect the current value changes.

Because of changing values, more public service employees do not see working in the public sector as distinct to working in the private sector. Instead, many public service professions are perceived as jobs and less as a vocation. However, work as such is still important for most people. Even more, individual performance orientation, life-long learning and the willingness to continuously adapt one's skills and competences have become new and positive values. Also workplace ethics have changed: In the past, the standard employment model meant that men worked full-time and stayed in their protected jobs until retirement. Workers were expected to erect a firewall between their work lives and their home lives. Today, the standard employment model is eroding, and the boundaries between the public and the private spheres are blurring. Also working time ethics (work from 9 A.M. to 5 P.M. in the office as being separated and closed off from home) have become relative, as employees can be reached on their smartphones anywhere and anytime. Moreover, an increasing number of employees work part-time, or according to flexible time arrangements. Yet, hard work is still seen as a virtue. In the past years, most European public employees have even seen their working hours increased. Early retirement and the 35-hour week is on the retreat. Many Member States apply the derogation clause in article 17 of the European Working Time Directive to their top-officials which allows for an extension of the working time above 48 hours per week.

Fast changes that are taking place can also be seen in the field of skill development, life-long learning and competency development. Whereas in the past civil servants were experts who held diplomas and received little training, today civil servants are required to continuously develop their skills and competencies. These fast-paced changes that are taking place in the field of competency development are typical of the entire field of workplace ethics. Today, no fixed workplace ethics exist. Instead, workplace ethics is continuously developing. And they change at an ever faster speed.

Today, the national public services are also becoming more exposed to outside organisational cultures and values. This does not suggest that the core public sector values – independent, merit based, professional, inclusive, responsive and fair – are going to disappear. However, the public services need to identify and emphasise the common ethical values that they share with other sectors.

"Next, the continuing emergence of new technologies and more diverse and informal means of communicating also raises challenging ethical issues. It means that the public services and other public sectors are increasingly going to have to use online communication, in particular, weblogs, or 'blogs', both to canvass community and stakeholder opinion in policy development and to provide information on policy and program implementation. New communication technology also means that individual public servants, both at work and outside it, are going to have access to, and possibly be tempted by, a range of different on line vehicles for self-expression – Facebook, YouTube, Wikipedia. The issue with online communication is the ease with which it can be accessed and speed and breadth with which it can spread, which means that one can never be certain of where and in what form it might end up. This means that the public sector ethical issues around communication – information versus advocacy, private versus public comment, misuse of resources to circulate partisan or offensive material – will become exponentially more challenging and costly to manage"[114].

According to the Australian Public Service Commissioner[115], there is a growing need for new detection methods on public comment and ICT use to cover blogs. "I am also conscious that there may need to be a shift in the way in which we perceive our rights and responsibilities in this information age. Our problems with the misuse of ICT – which in recent years have ranged from unauthorised browsing other people's personal records to accessing, storage and distribution of offensive and obscene material – appear to be, at least in part, a product of the longstanding practice that public servants are entitled to modest use of public resources for their own private purposes (...). Nonetheless, I remain very concerned that misuse of ICT occurs at all – either the fundamental message appears not to be getting through, or there is some sort of dissonance between people knowing how to behave but not being willing to do so. In future we will need to think about setting clearer and more consistent boundaries about private use and inappropriate use of the internet and of mobile devices, and this is likely to involve the commitment of resources for training and other awareness rising"[116].

114 Lynelle Briggs, Testing APS ethics, op. cit., p. 133.
115 Ibid., pp. 119–136
116 Ibid., p. 134

4. ETHICS POLICIES AND ETHICS MANAGEMENT

4.1 Ethics policies – focusing on inputs, rather than outcomes

Ethical standards matter in public and daily management practices. The ethical tone of a public organisation impacts its efficiency, effectiveness, decision-making processes, employee commitment and job satisfaction, employee stress and employee turnover. Making ethical practices a priority is not just about functioning with integrity or being credible, it is also about optimising the efficient functioning of public organisations. Public organisations that perform well are generally characterised by high ethical standards both externally, in their dealings with stakeholders, and internally, in relationships amongst the employees[117].

In the various European states, the political systems and political cultures differ according to factors such as the strength and scrutiny rights of parliament, party penetration of bureaucracies, freedom of the press, the size of administrations, the design of organisational structures and HR systems, etc. Despite all political and legal differences, it is widely accepted that public ethics can only flourish under conditions which are alike and the same – everywhere. For example, critical media, clear and transparent rules on party financing and a watchful parliament have a positive effect on ethics in the public sector. Almost all existing studies show that a high party penetration of the public sector is favouring patronage and favouritism, while a clear separation is fostering integrity[118]. It is also quite evident that the accountability of the public sector can be considerably strengthened through a parliament which takes its monitoring and controlling role seriously.

A further crucial factor in creating a favourable environment for an ethical public sector is the setting-up of an independent judiciary with effective accountability institutions such as an internal audit system, commissions of inquiry and an ombudsman. Independence in this context means that the heads of these institutions are subject to special non-political appointment and dismissal procedures, and that the management of human and financial resources enjoys sufficient independence. One weakness of these institutions, which is pointed out in the literature, is that they are not focused enough on the role of investigating breaches of integrity, but they tend to focus more on financial and performance

---

117 Ibid., pp. 119–136

118 See, for instance, Yves Mény /Martin Rhodes (1997), Illicit governance: Corruption, scandal and fraud, in: Martin Rhodes/Paul Heywood/Vincent Wright (Eds.), Developments in West European politics, Basingstoke 1997, pp. 95-105.

auditing.[119] Key requirements regarding the legal framework include the following:

- Independent and effective judiciary;
- Independent prosecution;
- Effective monitoring and implementation bodies, e.g. police;
- Sound complaint and recourse mechanisms.

The establishment of an ethical public sector is further encouraged by economic factors, such as a well-functioning market economy, a competitive, independent and ethical private sector and an advanced legal framework for public procurement. Moreover, effective ethics is supported by political processes which support ethics policies from the design of the policy or instrument to its implementation and enforcement.

Ideally, the decision-making process in the field of ethics policies can be defined, in all Member States, as a policy cycle or a political process in which ethics policies are designed, adopted, implemented, enforced and evaluated (see Figure 4 on page 55). The policy as such can be evaluated as to whether or not it has attained its objectives and according to its outcomes.

The input includes the agenda setting and the policy formulation phase, the adoption of rules and laws, principles and codes, models and instruments. The policy implementation phase includes all managerial and organisational tasks, including the distribution of roles, functions, coordination mechanisms, structures. The output includes monitoring, reporting and enforcement of policies, and includes all issues as regards the implementation of the input policies and the evaluation of policies.

---

119 See in this context for instance, Robert Schwartz, Breaches of integrity and accountability institutions: Auditors, anti-corruption agencies and commissions of inquiry. Paper presented at the meeting of the Study Group on Ethics and Integrity of Governance, Annual Conference of the European Group of Public Administration, September 2003, Oeiras, Portugal, p. 10 onwards. Concerning an investigation of supreme audit institutions (SAI) in several countries, the author comes to the conclusion that the proportion of total SAI resources devoted to the function of investigating breaches of integrity and the proportion of total findings that deal with integrity is quite small.

Figure 4. Ethics policies from a policy cycle approach[120]

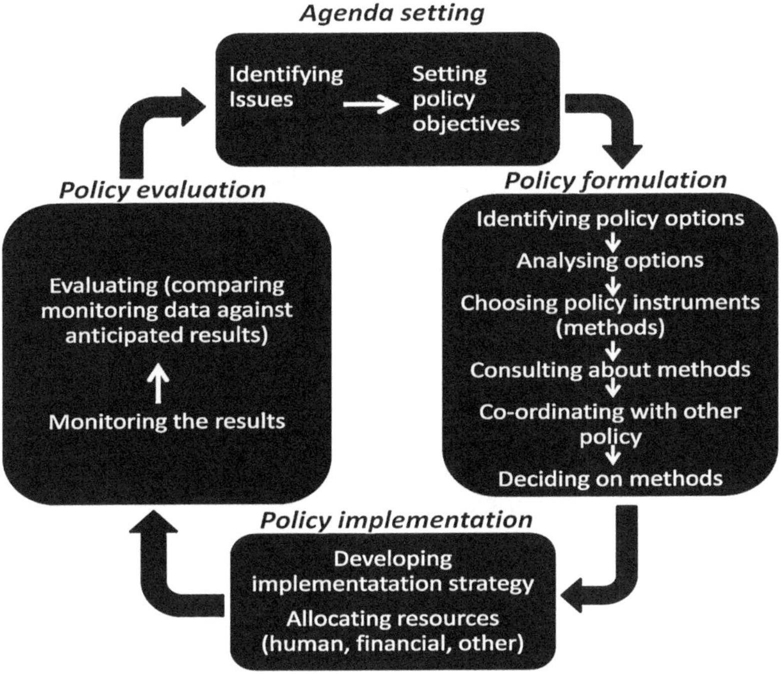

In the field of ethics, in many Member States the focus has been on the input of ethics policies (including the agenda setting process and the policy formulation, until the adoption of rules). However, in some of the more advanced countries another trend took place. For example, in the Netherlands the focus has been less on the adoption of new rules, policies, instruments and controls during the last years. Instead, more resources have been invested in the so-called soft instruments such as investments in competency and skill development of employees, training on ethical dilemmas and the increase of ethical consciousness[121].

Politicians and public managers typically approach ethics from the utilitarian perspective. They try to make ethical decisions that benefit the greatest number of citizens, voters or employees. "The political climate is now more favourable

---

120 http://www.mfe.govt.nz/publications/rma/drafting-issues-jul03/html/page2.html, last time checked on 26.3.2012.

121 J.H.J. van den Heuvel/Leo Huberts/Zeger van der Wal/K. Steenburgen, Integriteit van het lokaal bestuur, Boom, 2010, p. 89.

for ethics – or at least for talk about ethics (…). One reason for the growing respectability of ethics is, no doubt, that politicians have discovered that moral talk, and sometimes even moral action, helps them win or stay in office"[122].

During the last decades, ethics laws and policies have become more numerous and stricter. However, this can be also interpreted as a sign for ethics being a highly symbolic policy. In fact, as we will see later on, ethics policies are mostly scandal-driven but ethics is not an important policy. Another problem concerns the fact that ethics policies are increasingly overloaded with expectations. Today, ethics policies should not only provide a tool for identifying, preventing and resolving ethical challenges. Instead, they should also:

- Increase public confidence in the government;
- Demonstrate the high level of integrity of the vast majority of Government officials;
- Deter conflicts of interest from arising, as official activities would be subject to public scrutiny;
- Better enable the public to judge the performance of public officials in the light of their outside financial interests.

How are ethics becoming a political issue? According to our findings, the main cause in most countries is media coverage. Also international organisations such as the OECD and GRECO within the Council of Europe have played an important role in bringing the topic on the agenda. Still, politicians and civil servants play a minor role in bringing "ethics" on the agenda. Even more, it is still difficult to report ethical problems, both, within the political system and within the administration.

At the same time, ethics policies are adopted in a very dynamic external context. For example, whereas only some decades ago homosexuality was seen problematic and not in conformity with moral standards, today it is widely accepted. Thus, ethics and moral policies change as norms and values are changing. Despite the quickly changing perceptions of moral attitudes and ethics, increasingly, ethics policies have become a relatively stable and more important feature in politics. In fact, ethics have become a political instrument as such. However, the implementation of ethics policies is not taken seriously. How can this paradox be explained?

According to Denis Martin, politicians "keep on adopting more ethics rules because: a) this is the proper thing to do in a democracy; b) it is politically difficult

---

122 Gutman/Thompson, op. cit., p. ix.

to be against more ethics; c) because ethics rules provide easily accessible resources for political combat; d) they also provide symbolic reassurance against misconduct; and e) they are cheap to adopt because enforcement is weak"[123]. Since ethics policies are mostly scandal-driven, politicians and managers are less interested in the policy process that follows the decision-making process. In our study, only one country, the Netherlands, reported that public discussions on ethics are mostly value-driven.

Table 2. Are public discussions on ethics value-driven or scandal-driven? (N=26)

(Frequencies in parentheses)

	Old Member States	New Member States	Total
Value-driven ++	0 (0)	0 (0)	0 (0)
Value-driven +	7 (1)	0 (0)	4 (1)
Hard to say	29 (4)	58 (7)	42 (11)
Scandal-driven -	43 (6)	33 (4)	39 (10)
Scandal-drive --	21 (3)	8 (1)	15 (4)
Total	199 (14)	100 (12)	100 (26)

In fact, the dominance of scandal-driven policies also means that popular ethics are more discussed than other issues. For example, discussions on corruption are far more popular than discussions on post-employment issues or mobbing.

123 Denis Saint-Martin, Path dependence and self-reinforcing process, in: Denis Saint-Martin/Fred Thompson (Eds.), Public ethics and governance, op. cit., p. 17.

Table 3. Public discussions on public-service ethics in EU-27

(1=no, 2=somewhat, 3=intensive)

	Old Member States	New Member States
Post-employment issues related to civil servants	1,50	1,83
Discrimination	1,57	2,25
Unethical behaviour in general	1,67	1,82
Conflict of interest issues related to civil servants	1,71	2,33
Mobbing	1,71	1,67
Post-employment issues related to politicians	1,79	1,92
Misuse of organisational resources	1,86	2,08
Core values (e.g., openness)	1,86	2,17
Administrative corruption	2,07	2,42
Misconduct	2,08	2,17
Ethical standards	2,21	2,00
Conflict of interest issues related to politicians	2,64	2,42
Political corruption	2,64	2,75

As Table 3 indicates, discussions on public-service ethics mostly concern political corruption and conflict of interest issues related to politicians. Public debates on administrative corruption and conflict of interest issues related to civil servants seem to occur less often. According to the responses, public discussions on ethics seem to be more frequent among the New Member States.

Still, ethics policies are not only scandal-driven. This widely held belief contradicts the fact that ethics policies differ from country to country. This suggests that policies are also influenced by the different political, cultural and institutional features. Moreover, what has also often been overlooked is the different institutional context in which ethical decisions are made: existing values, leadership, organisational culture, the effects of working conditions on behaviour, organisational structures, etc. Furthermore, there is a huge difference between ethics policies and ethics management. Whereas the former is highly symbolic, the latter is increasingly complex and technical. Often ethics policies and management issues are in conflict. For example, implementing and managing the principle of impartiality can conflict with political and economic interests.

Consequently, too little has been done as regards the outcome of ethics policies and the evaluation of ethics policies. This can be seen in the context of cost evaluations: almost all Member States reported that they have never undertaken any evaluations as regards the costs of ethics policies. Overall, there is also little evidence as to the outcomes of different instruments in the field of ethics. For example, what have been the outcomes of anti-gift policies? Are they more effective than strict post-employment rules?

What is the relation between the input of ethics policies and their output and outcome? It is often assumed that more and better rules in the field of ethics and more issues covered by ethics policies should – at least in theory – lead to more trust, greater accountability, more integrity and less unethical behaviour/corruption. This should be done by improving the throughput, e.g. credible enforcement systems, effective ethics management systems, ethical leadership, ethical cultures and stable values that endure over time.

Finally, what do we know about the major obstacles and difficulties for an effective ethics policy? Our study reveals some important answers to this question. As can be discerned from Table 4, most Member States responded that ethics policies are not taken seriously, and there is not enough awareness and knowledge of public-service ethics[124]. This is the case especially in the new Member States. Also the lack of active leadership and leadership commitment as well as problems related to the enforcement of ethics codes were mentioned as an obstacle for an effective ethics policy.

---

124 On the other hand, an earlier study for the Slovenian EU-Presidency indicated that 45.4% of the public employees were of the opinion that ethical rules are better known than before, whereas 19.4% of respondents disagreed with that statement. See Demmke/Henökl/Moilanen, What are public services good at? op. cit.

Table 4. Major obstacles and difficulties for an effective ethics policy

(1= major obstacle, 2=minor obstacle, 3= not an obstacle)

	Old Member States	New Member States	Total
Ethics policies are not taken seriously – not enough awareness and knowledge of ethics rules	1,86	1,42	1,65
Lack of active leadership and leadership commitment	1,93	1,58	1,77
Enforcement of codes (if codes exist)	2,07	1,78	1,96
Ethics policies are not integrated into other policies (e.g. through unfair recruitment, pay, promotion policies)	2,07	1,83	1,96
No monitoring (registration of ethical violations lacking)	2,00	2,00	2,00
Lack of ethics-related training	2,00	2,08	2,04
Organisational culture does not match with ethical standards	2,14	2,00	2,08
No independent ethics examinations (e.g., through ethics commissions)	2,21	1,92	2,08
Lack of sanctions/deterrence	2,14	2,00	2,08
Lack of evaluation of violations	2,21	1,92	2,08
HRM policy is not strictly merit-based (exceptions for politicians, top-managers, public employees, minorities, women, disabled persons)	2,29	2,17	2,23
HRM policy contradicts with ethical requirements (no independent selection and recruitment procedures, politicized administration, control of diplomas and references, no review list of vulnerable functions, oath etc.)	2,43	2,17	2,31
Poor quality of existing laws, regulations and codes	2,50	2,42	2,46

Evaluation of ethics policies is complicated. So far, there is still too little empirical evidence as to the output and outcomes of ethics policies. What is known relates to the poor implementation and enforcement of ethics policies. For example, we know that many deficiencies result from the fact that ethics policies are not supported by credible enforcement systems and effective ethics management systems. This means that ethical standards seem to exist on paper but they are not translated into real life policies. On the other hand, ethical scandals are too often blamed on the lack of adequate controls over decisions and actions. In this use of the term, control is equated with the mainly negative purpose of preventing wrongdoing. Rules, hierarchy, reporting, monitoring and sanctions to enforce compliance are the means used to achieve the aim of preventing abuse or mistakes.

4.2 Ethics management – the quest for the right approach

Literature on managerial ethics[125] focuses mainly on the private sector. In fact, public-service ethics differs in some, but not in all, aspects from the business ethics. For example, in both sectors, the key actors are the same: top-management, line management, the HR department, the financial administration and the integrity officials. Moreover, the pre-conditions for an effective ethics management are the same: the existence of policies, strategies, plans, instruments, (financial) resources and budgets, expertise and knowledge.

Despite these common features, differences also exist. Firstly, "(t)here is a fundamental difference between the public sector and the private sector. Citizens can choose whether to buy private sector products and services and they can choose whether and where they want to invest their money. But they must all, in one way or another, pay taxes and they are all affected, in one way or another, by decisions of the government. The *quid pro quo* for this is that citizens in our democracy are entitled to, and expect, a particularly high standard of stewardship of the resources – intellectual, personnel, material and financial – that they have granted the public sector. Their expectations include that:

• these resources will be managed effectively and that their use will be accounted for;

• they will not be used for partisan political purposes or for personal advantage; and

• the standards of behaviour of the people paid to manage these resources should be beyond reproach and meet or be better than the standards in other sectors"[126].

Secondly, ethics management in the public sector[127] is more constrained and also influenced by the legal and organisational context. Targets and strategic

---

125 Marshall Schmink (Ed.), Managerial ethics, Routledge, New York, 2010.
126 Lynelle Briggs, Testing APS Ethics, op. cit., p. 119.

choices are heavily influenced by political considerations. Also HR management in the public sector differs from private sector HR management, in the sense that different rules and standards are applied and must be taken into consideration (especially as regards the legal status, duty to take an oath, existence of specific requirements in the recruitment process, etc.)[128].

Thirdly, public employees are required to develop different competencies than private sector employees, since their first task is to serve the public interest and to respect the law. According to Menzel, an ethical government manager is 1) committed to high standards of personal and professional behaviour, 2) has knowledge of relevant ethics codes and laws, 3) has the ability to engage in ethical reasoning when confronted with challenging situations, 4) is able to identify and act on public service ethics and values, and 5) promotes ethical practices and behaviour in public agencies and organisations[129].

Still, ethics management in the public and private sector share a number of common features. It has been suggested that in order to be effective, ethics management must fulfil the following preconditions[130]:

- There must be a management vision;
- There must be a central actor with responsibilities in the field of ethics;
- There must be clear targets and objectives;
- The concrete ethics policies must be consistent with the targets,
- The choice of instruments must be coherent;
- Ethics policies must be continually communicated;
- Ethics policies must be continually evaluated.

Similarly to the private sector, ethical management in the public sector is a typical horizontal policy. Its success depends mostly on the integration of ethics policies into other policies, organisational values, guidance, communication, awareness raising and prevention. Consequently, the main task of ethics management is not only to penalise wrongdoings, but to prevent them from happening and to encourage proper behaviour by guidance and orientation measures, such as training and the introduction of codes of conducts.

---

127 See Bossaert/Demmke, Main challenges in the field of ethics and integrity in the EU Member States, op. cit.

128 Hal G. Rainey, Understanding and managing public organistions, Third Edition, Jossey Bass, San Francisco, 2003.

129 Donald Menzel, Ethics moments in government, CRC Press, Boca Raton, 2010, p. 18.

130 W.N. Dunn, Public policy analysis: An introduction, Fourth Edition, Upper Saddle River, NJ: Pearson/Prentice Hall, 2008; A. Hoogerwerf & M. Herweijer, Overheidsbeleid: Een inleiding in de beleidswetenschap, Kluwer, Alphen aan den Rijn, 2008.

Research on ethics management in the European public sector appeared late and was motivated by the early OECD studies on trust and ethics infrastructures[131]. Here, public ethics management was defined as "a systematic and conscious effort to promote organisational integrity" in public organisations[132]. According to the OECD, a sound integrity framework should fulfil four important functions, namely: (a) determining and defining integrity, (b) guiding towards integrity, (c) monitoring integrity, and (d) enforcing integrity.

The OECD approach has always stressed that an effective ethics infrastructure should at the same time aim to control (through a qualitative legislative framework and effective accountability and control institutions), guide (through codes of conducts and professional socialisation) and manage (through fair public service conditions and an overall coordinating body) civil servants. Furthermore, the OECD also stresses the key role of commitment by political leadership.

Table 5. Typology of integrity management instruments[133]

<table>
<tr><th></th><th>(a)Determining and defining</th><th>(b) Guiding</th><th>(c) Monitoring</th><th>(d) Enforcing</th></tr>
<tr><td>Core</td><td>➢ risk analysis
➢ codes of conduct/ codes of ethics
➢ conflict of interest policy
➢ gifts and hospitality policy
➢ post-employment arrangements
➢ structural arrangements (e.g.: staff rotation for sensitive posts)
➢ analysis of ethical dilemmas
➢ consultation of staff and stakeholders</td><td>● integrity/ ethics training
● oath, signing an "integrity declaration"
● specialized information and advice for staff
➢ integrating ethics issues in regular communication channels
➢ exemplary behaviour by management</td><td>➢ whistleblowing[14] policy
➢ complaints policy
➢ inspections
➢ integrity testing
➢ survey measurement of integrity violations and organizational climate
➢ probing for ethical dilemmas and issues among staff</td><td rowspan="2">➢ formal sanctions
➢ fair and appropriate procedures for handling investigations
➢ communication about integrity violations
➢ informal sanctions</td></tr>
<tr><td>Complementary</td><td colspan="2">➢ assessing the fairness of reward and promotion systems
➢ appropriate procedures for procurement, contract mgt. and payment
➢ measures in personnel mgt. (e.g.: integrity as a criterion for selection, promotion etc.)
➢ measures in financial control (e.g.: "double key", transparency of financial information)
➢ measures in information mgt (e.g.: protecting automated databases)</td><td>➢ internal control and audit
➢ external control and audit</td></tr>
</table>

131 Ibid.

132 Donald Menzel, Research on ethics and integrity in governance: A review and assessment, in; Public Integrity, Vol. 7, No. 2/2005, pp. 147–168.

133 OECD, Towards a sound integrity framework: Instruments, processes, structures, and conditions for implementation, Paris, 2009.

The compliance –integrity continuum[134] is still the principal analytical device for categorizing various approaches to ethics management. In fact, it distinguishes between two different legal and administrative styles and approaches which are currently applied: a compliance-based approach and a value-based approach. In both cases, the objective is ultimately the same: to foster high levels of ethical behaviour[135]. However, no Member State uses a pure approach. Whereas some rely more on a compliance-based approach, others focus on preventative approaches. The right combination has yet to be established. Thus, for example, Germany represents a relatively strong compliance-based approach[136]. Other countries, e.g. the United Kingdom apply a mixture between a compliance based, preventative and a value-based approach.

Each approach has its own challenges. A compliance-based approach has to deal with the strengths and weaknesses of pure rule-based ethics. For instance, this approach tends to develop elaborate codes emphasising compliance with rules, thus acquiring a strong legalistic tendency[137]." Since this is the case in Germany, it is quite straightforward to foster relatively high standards of ethics. In this approach, problems may occur when people tend to think that if something is not explicitly prohibited, then it is not wrong[138]. Another weakness is that legalistic approaches help eliminate and prevent "the most serious trespasses, but they do not go far enough in promoting positive ethical attitudes and behaviour. Consequently, organisations that rely on them are vulnerable to a dramatic increase in unethical behaviour as soon as members of the organisation perceive the enforcement levels to be dropping"[139].

The value-based approach emphasises informal instruments and values that underlie the rules made by government for the management of public resources. In this way, it goes beyond a pure rule-based approach. However, although a pre-

---

134 See OECD, Ethics in the public service, op. cit. and OECD, Trust in government, op. cit.; originally by Lynn Sharp Paine, Managing for organizational integrity, Harvard Business Review, 1994.

135 National Defence of Canada, Fundamentals of Canadian defence ethics, defence ethics program, January 2002, p. 3.

136 For example, see Robert Michkowitz, Corruption in law enforcement agencies – views from within the criminal justice system: Results from a German corruption study, in: Cyrille Fijnaut/Leo Huberts, Corruption, integrity and law enforcement, Kluwer Law International, 2002, pp. 75-90; Barbara Huber, Sanctions against bribery offences in criminal law, in: Fijnaut/Huberts, Corruption, integrity and law enforcement, op. cit., pp. 137-151.

137 National Defence of Canada, op. cit., p. 4.

138 Ibid.

139 Ibid.

ventative-based approach stresses the values that will promote positive ethical behaviour, it remains tied to specific functional areas of the organisation. Paradoxically, its strength is also its limitation. By concentrating on the development of ethical competencies, values and virtues, this approach neglects the importance and effects of deterrent mechanisms and formal instruments. Often, it also overemphasises the possibility of virtue approaches (the possibility to change behaviour by learning ethics) and underestimates the importance of external (economic factors) factors on individual behaviour.

There is a common understanding that both approaches are too broad and not sufficient to foster integrity, and that they must be supplemented by a more active approach which considers ethical behaviour a consequence of factors such as good working conditions, fair salaries, an open and motivating working atmosphere, well-functioning and active communication at all levels, and model role playing by political and administrative leaders. In fact, whatever approach is chosen, ultimately, the effectiveness of ethics management depends on the effectiveness of different instruments in different administrative contexts.

A Dutch study[140] which concerned the effectiveness of 21 anti-corruption strategies is of general relevance for all countries. In this study, too, it is interesting to see the key role given to the administrative and political management. In this sense, 86.9% are of the opinion that more commitment by politicians is a key variable to combat unethical behaviour (internal control and supervision: 86.5%). It is also rather revealing – but also logical – that the variable "example given by management at the top" (80%) also scores relatively high. On the other hand, more severe penal sanctions (64.2%) and extension of police and judiciary (57.1%) are also important instruments, but were mentioned less among the experts. Other instruments are characterised by their relative significance in the fight against corruption: public information campaigns (71.6%); code of ethics for politicians and civil servants (73.1%); better protection for whistleblowers (74.2%) and stronger selection of public personnel (73.2%).

---

140 Leo Huberts, What can be done against public corruption and fraud? Expert views on strategies to protect public integrity, in: Crime, Law & Social Change, Vol. 29, 2-3/1998, pp. 209-224.

Table 6. Expert panel views on effectiveness of 21 anti-corruption methods (percentage of respondents considering the method very effective)

Strategy	Higher income country (opinions of 190 experts)
Economic	
Reasonable standard of living	50.0%
Higher salaries for politicians/public servants	34.4%
Less government/privatisation	27.9%
Making banking and finance more transparent	69.9%
Educational	
Public information campaigns	71.6%
More public exposure	76.6%
Changing family attitudes	37.1%
Influencing attitudes of public servants	76.8%
Public culture	
Example given by senior management	80.0%
Code of ethics for politicians and civil servants	73.1%
Better protection for whistle blowers	74.2%
Organisational/bureaucratic	
Rotation of personnel	51.6%
Internal control and supervision	86.5%
Improved selection of public personnel	73.2%
Political	
More commitment by politicians	86.9%
Transparency regarding party finances	80.3%
Example given by senior management	80.0%
Greater division of public powers	48.4%
Less government/privatisation	27.9%
Repressive/judicial	
More severe penal measures	64.2%
Extension of police and judiciary	57.1%
Creating independent institutions	75.1%
Combating organised crime	77.3%
Making banking and finance more transparent	69.6%

Still, huge differences exist between the normative idea, the conviction that ethical leadership is important, and the daily administrative reality which often limits the possibility to act clearly and in accordance with leadership theories. Consequently, Mintzberg[141] differentiates between managers and leaders. The possibility to exercise leadership is limited by a number of managerial tasks. Therefore, most leaders are rather mangers than leaders. Lewis and Gilman describe the role of managers: "The public manager must act quickly in a grey, marginal area where laws are silent or confusing, circumstances are ambiguous and complex, and the manager is responsible, well-meaning, and perplex"[142]. Daily management leaves little time to brainstorm and to think about dilemmas. Often, long working days and time pressure put additional stress on the manager's shoulders "In fact, managers make most of their ethical choices this way: in the pit of the stomach, automatically, reflexively, intuitively in the popular sense, by common sense…"[143]. Mostly, managers dismiss theoretical concepts and philosophical traditions in the field of ethics as artificial and impractical. For managers, the sheer number and complexity of ethical traditions will not make the management of daily life issues easier. "As a result, the obligation of informed ethical reasoning – thinking through a dilemma and making a morally reasonable decision – falls on the individual public manager"[144].

The consequences of this (unprofessional) way of dealing with ethical issues and the lack of ethical leadership leads to the discrepancy between theory and practice. For example, a study on "Integriteit van de Overheid"[145] (Integrity of the Government), which was commissioned by the Dutch Ministry of the Interior in 2007, revealed that relatively high percentages of public employees were relatively dissatisfied with issues such as ethical leadership, ethical awareness raising and ethical culture. From here, one should conclude that practical ethics training and dilemma training is important for leaders despite all practical limitations in the daily managerial life and scarce of time for managers.

4.2.1 Designing the right incentives

The notion that public organisations and their leaders should be held accountable for the success of their organisations and rewarded accordingly is largely

---

141 Henry Mintzberg, Managing, San Francisco, 2009.

142 Carol W. Lewis/Stuart C. Gilman, The ethics challenge in public service: A problem-solving guide, Jossey-Bass, second edition, 2005.

143 Ibid.

144 Carol W. Lewis/Stuart C. Gilman, The ethics challenge in public service, op. cit.

145 Ministerie van Binnenlandse Zaken en Koningsrijkrelaties, Integriteit van de Overheid, Den Hague, 2007.

missing in ethics debates. This negative orientation has the potential to lead to the neglect of the prospect of ethics as a learning process, involving the remediation of problems. Moreover, if we wish to employ sanctioning systems as viable and effective tools of ethical behaviour, more research is needed to investigate how the presence of sanctions can also shape people´s intrinsic moral incentives[146]. Traditionally, ethics management had focused on rule obedience and sanctions. Whereas research on sanctions and punishment has advanced significantly in the field of ethics[147], discussions on rewards and incentives that promote ethical conduct are almost absent. Nobody receives a bonus for ethical leadership or exemplary conduct.

Still, it is not clear what types of rewards work best to encourage responsible and accountable behaviour, including the search for improvement. In theory, in order to establish appropriate incentives to promote efficiency and effectiveness, as well as disincentives to prevent abuses and unethical behaviour, a balanced ethics regime should involve a range of positive and negative consequences.

Today, most public services provide only for different sanctions in cases of misconduct, wrongdoing or unethical behaviour. The most classical instrument is the use of disciplinary actions and the dismissal a public official in the case of serious wrongdoings. In fact, disciplinary sanctions are only used in a very limited number of cases. Over the past years more employers have also introduced the option to sanction employees in cases of poor performance. As a consequence, people will not be promoted or do not get performance-related bonuses. However, it is questionable whether this instrument is effective in the field of ethics. The social and organisational justice literature suggests that subordinates' reactions to sanctions are based on justice evaluations that consider the perceived fairness of outcomes (distributive justice), of punishment, the processes by which outcome decisions are made (procedural justice), and the interpersonal treatment received (interactional justice). Thus, the question how punishment and sanctions are administered matters greatly if punishment and sanctions are to be effective. Moreover, justice evaluations are extremely important to employees' reactions[148].

---

146 David de Creer, On the psychology of preventing and dealing with ethical failures: A behavioural ethics approach, in: Marshall Schimanke (Ed.), Managerial ethics, op. cit., p. 116.

147 Klebe/Trevino/Weaver, Advances in research on punishment in organisations: Descriptive and normative perspectives, in: Marshall Schimanke (Ed.), Managerial ethics, op. cit., p. 198.

148 Ibid., p. 180.

Sanctions and punishments have only minor effects in many fields of counterproductive work behaviour[149] or insidious workplace behaviour[150]. This poses a problem as counterproductive work behaviour represents a considerable challenge in an organisation and the impact of ongoing unethical conduct and poor performance is rather high as these persons:

- do not deliver required business outcomes or value for money;
- impair the standard, reputation and professionalism of the Civil Service;
- disrupt the flow of work and increase the workloads of their colleagues;
- cause resentment and lower morale; and
- set a bad example to those they manage.

There is no doubt that staff becomes unmotivated and even cynical when unethical behaviour is not dealt with. While inadequate recognition of good performance is often a cause of concern, the inability of an organisation to manage ineffectiveness and poor performance creates even stronger resentment and affects the credibility of the whole organisation.

A central challenge of managing counterproductive behaviour results from the fact that many things inside and outside the workplace can affect an individual's motivation and performance. Important reasons for this behaviour may be a lack of incentives, unclear tasks and objectives, bad leadership, ability, skills and motivation, unethical behaviour of colleagues, misfit between job expectations and job tasks, etc. Managing counterproductive work behaviour has to be understood as a key leadership task. A good manager will identify the reasons and discuss them with the person concerned in order to find out what can be done to improve the situation. In many cases communication, training or coaching may be sufficient. Managers should also be sensitive to other factors such as stress, relationship problems and financial difficulties. Albeit managers cannot resolve such issues, they should do their best to bring performance back to an acceptable level.

It is also important to recognise that some reasons for unethical behaviour are understandable, while others are not. In the meantime, literature on reasons, means and motives of insidious and counterproductive workplace behaviour[151] has greatly advanced. Still, more research is needed especially in the field of workplace stress and its impact on workplace behaviour. As it seems, psycho-

---

149 Suzy Fox/ Paul E. Spector (Eds.), Counterproductive work behaviour, Washington D.C., 2005.

150 Jerald Greenberg, Insidious workplace behaviour, Routledge, 2010.

151 Greenberg, Insidious Workplace Behaviour, op. cit.; Fox/Spector, op. cit.

logical disorders and stress-related diseases are on the increase. In fact, the increase of psychological stress has a great impact on workplace behaviour[152]. There is also a difference between a short-term decline of behavioural standards and consecutive periods of poor conduct. The longer unethical conduct is allowed to linger, the greater the problem for the individuals and organisation when it is finally tackled.

The inability to adequately handle the underlying reasons of counterproductive work behaviour and unethical conduct is regarded as a central obstacle for many managers in many organisations. There is a substantial awareness of the fact that managers often do not have adequate means to sanction this behaviour and that the assessment system often does not provide the clear message to the employees that this behaviour is not tolerated.

4.2.2 Self-assessment tools or audits

Self-assessment tools and/or audits are good preventive instruments for organisations. Self-assessment tools are appraisals, "the purpose being to determine if changes need to be made in the climate, environment, codes, and the enforcement of ethics policies"[153]. An ethics audit is not an accounting or financial management audit. In most cases organisations offer their employees to provide confidential information about the ethical climate in their organisation. The purpose of this instrument is to link results concerning the ethical climate in an organisation with the values of efficiency, effectiveness, quality, trust, etc.

Increasingly, these audits or assessments are offered as self-scans on the Internet or intranet. It is difficult to assess the effectiveness of these self-assessments and audit tools. One should also not forget that these instruments can easily turn bureaucratic. Employees may be critical, because they may be concerned with control issues and concerns about the protection of their privacy. But these concerns should be "weighed carefully in light of the organisational pay-offs, increased productivity, greater work satisfaction, lower turnover rates of personnel, and the building of public trust and confidence in the agency. There are other important reasons to conduct an ethics audit. An audit can identify gaps in policies and procedures, including gaps in the need to increase awareness of areas of potential ethical risk"[154].

---

152 Alain Ehrenberg, La societe du malaise, op. cit.

153 Donald Menzel, Ethics management for public administrators, Sharpe, Armonk, 2007, p. 72.

154 Ibid., p. 74.

4.2.3 Managing conflicts of interests

Legislation in the EU Member States and the European Commission includes measures that strengthen the core civil service values of impartiality, neutrality, integrity and openness, and which are aimed at preventing a collusion of private interests with the exercise of public duties. In this sense, conflicts of interest regulations constitute a specialised code applicable only to public officials and Holders of Public Office[155]. These regulations are characterised by high standards of morality that go much further than the standard to which private employees would normally be expected to adhere. Their goal is not to punish wrongdoing, but to provide safeguards which lessen the risk of undesirable action[156]. In this context, legal provisions consist of a list of "shall nots" and are being put into place because each public sector employee – in addition to being a civil servant – is a shareholder, a member of an association or simply a relative of a director of a tax consultancy.

In many respects, relations between the public and the private sector are very sensitive and give cause for unethical behaviour. With the increased contacts between the two sectors due to the increasing trend towards private-public partnerships, conflicts of interest situations are becoming more frequent. Nonetheless, it is difficult to find evidence of a resulting increase in corruption and fraud. The responses to the questionnaire illustrate no clear trend in this respect: half of the EU Member States perceive the increased mobility between the two sectors as being vulnerable to integrity violations (a third of the countries responded "hard to say").

According to an OECD study, the main sources of conflicts of interest in OECD countries are (1) secondary employment in the private sector; (2) private-public partnerships, and (3) shareholdings in an entity with a contractual or regulatory relationship with the government[157]. With regard to the instruments to be considered in preventing conflicts of interest, the responses showed a combination of mechanisms that raise awareness and ensure transparency. In addition, more and more OECD countries are actively engaging in counselling and requesting disclosure of interests in writing, so that potential situations may be identified. Although we should not underestimate the significance of these instruments with

155 Demmke et al., Regulating conflicts of interest for Holders of Public Office in the European Union, op. cit.

156 On this topic, see for instance Frank Anechiarico/James B. Jacobs, The pursuit of absolute integrity, Chicago and London, 1996, pp. 45-63.

157 Janos Bertok, Managing conflicts of interest in OECD countries, in: Transparency International, Global corruption report 2003, p. 320.

regard to creating a more open and transparent public sector, we have to say that they only become effective when the management of this information is guaranteed systematically and continuously. Otherwise, these instruments will only serve to explain or provide insight into an act of fraud after it has been committed.

The extent of the interest to be disclosed differs from country to country. It may range from a pecuniary interest to a personal non-pecuniary interest, such as membership in different charity organisations. The difficulty is in defining the interest which may raise an ethical problem. The declaration of private interests in a register is the most common mechanism for dealing with conflicts of interest. "The popularity of this mechanism seems due in part to the ease of implementation and the clear message it sends of a commitment to transparency in government"[158]. Essentially, this mechanism requires the periodic declaration of all prescribed interests to a register of interests. In Ireland, for example, a number of public officials are required to declare any income (also of his/her family) in a register or to undertake a tax clearance obligation (for the Attorney-General and senior officials)[159]. However, registers of interests are not accepted everywhere. For example, some countries believe that registers are in conflict with fundamental rights (rights to privacy, personal rights, family rights, etc.).

It can also be observed that governments in general are placing a growing emphasis on conflict of interest regulations by introducing a greater diversity of rules in this field to their civil service laws. The answers to this study suggest that many states are increasingly striving for a high degree of transparency with regard to the private lives of public officials. In Ireland, for example, specific information requirements have been introduced. These requirements include an obligation to register additional jobs, private income or shares, or an obligation to provide information about the jobs/activities of the partner, which may be in conflict with the civil servant's position. Other rules refer to the acceptance of gifts and invitations, in order to prevent unwanted external influence on decision making. This may include a dinner offered by a private firm or accepting a gift, which can involve a holiday tour to some attractive places offered by an applicant in a public procurement procedure, or a small present offered to a civil servant working in the environment administration when giving a presentation for a firm in the field of solar energy.

---

158 Gerard Carney, Conflict of interest: Legislators, ministers and public officials, Transparency International Working Paper, 1998.

159 Standards in Public Office Commission, Guidelines on compliance with the provisions of the ethics in public office acts, 1995 and 2001, Dublin, January 2003.

As noted above, a secondary job in the private sector may constitute a conflict of interest. Consequently, a tax official working simultaneously as a tax consultant undoubtedly faces more conflict of interest situations compared to the situation where he only performs his public duties. In order to avoid such high-level risks and to guarantee the loyal, neutral and proper exercise of public duties, the majority of states have introduced some restrictions on additional activities. Ancillary jobs mean paid work or duties which the civil servant is entitled to refuse, in any profession, trade or business. For example, in Finland the State Civil Servants' Act states that a civil servant may not be disqualified for his/her own duties by an ancillary job, and the ancillary job must not endanger confidence in his/her impartiality to perform official duties or otherwise hamper the proper performance of the duties. A civil servant may not hold an ancillary job which requires his/her working hours to be spent handling the duties of the said job, unless the authority concerned grants them permission. Furthermore, civil servants shall report any other ancillary jobs to the authority, who may forbid them on the same grounds as when considering whether to grant permission for an ancillary job.

4.3 Institutionalisation of ethics policies and the management challenge: the case of disclosure policies and ethics bodies

The institutionalization of ethics is one important component of the management of ethics. It means implementing, enforcing and managing ethics formally and informally, and implementing them into daily administrative life through a variety of means and instruments. While the Member States have been increasingly active in the field of ethics rules and ethics regulations, this has often necessitated the need to establish new institutional structures and ethics bureaucracies. In the following chapters we will discuss two examples: the setting up and management of disclosure policies, and the establishment of ethics bodies, commissions and ethics committees. Our aim will be to assess the effectiveness of these measures.

4.3.1 Disclosure policies for Holders of Public Office and top public officials

During the last years disclosure policies have become one of the most important instruments in conflict of interest policies. The principle of proactive disclosure, i.e. that information must be publicly available prior to public request, is seen as important in achieving greater accountability, transparency and openness in government. The public availability of information disclosed by top decision makers is also seen as important to reinforce trust in government At present, more Member States apply the principle of disclosure to Holders of Public Office and public officials in the field of conflicts of interests. According to

OECD, paid outside positions are the most regulated private interests across the three branches of government[160].

Countries also increasingly require disclosure of private interests (mostly as regards outside positions and gifts) by officials in at-risk areas, such as tax and customs officials, procurement officers and financial authorities. Yet, nearly all OECD member countries make disclosed information only partially public. The data further shows that the prevention of conflict of interest in at-risk areas focuses primarily on the disclosure and prohibition of outside positions and gifts[161].

As can be seen from Table 7, our findings show that 92% of all politicians and 77% of all top officials are required to disclose financial interests. Whereas some Member States have very detailed disclosure requirements, others require much less information, which can even be provided on a voluntary basis (Denmark, Sweden, Netherlands). For example, in the Netherlands elected and appointed officials are obliged by law to make public the financial compensations they receive for ancillary activities. In Denmark, for Members of Parliament (Folketingsmedlemmer) it is voluntary to disclose their financial interests to a special register (Hvervsregister). For Members of Government, disclosure of own and spouse's financial interests is required according to a political decision.

Table 7. Financial disclosure concerning elected officials, top civil servants and other appointed officials

(Frequencies in parentheses)

	Elected officials	Top civil servants	Other appointed officials
Required	93 (25)	78 (21)	52 (13)
Not required	7 (2)	22 (6)	48 (12)
Total	100 (27)	100 (27)	100 (25)

In Ireland, all parliamentarians are required to disclose annually their personal interests including financial interests. Office holders must disclose additionally the interests (including financial interests), of which the office holder has actual knowledge, of a spouse or civil partner, a child or a child of a spouse. Every other person to whom the Ethics Acts apply (i.e. the Attorney-General; directors of state bodies and agencies; designated employees and special advisers) is re-

160 OECD, Government at a glance, op. cit., p. 209.
161 Ibid., p. 210.

quired to disclose the interests of the person, and the interests, of which the person has actual knowledge, of his or her spouse or civil partner or a child of the person or of his or her spouse, that could materially influence the person in his or her official duties. This includes financial interests. Financial interests comprise a holding by the person concerned of shares, bonds, debentures, or other similar investments in any particular company or other enterprise or undertaking, with an aggregate nominal or market value in excess of €13,000. Holding does not include money in a current, deposit or other similar account but does include a holding in unit trusts or managed funds. This disclosure would be made in the person's annual statement of interests. In Lithuania, public disclosure duties do not only concern financial interests, but also any other kind of private interests. In France and in Germany, only Members of Government and Members of Parliament are obliged to disclose their income declarations and patrimonial assets.

Other differences concern the degree of openness (public disclosure or internal disclosure), and questions of sanctioning if members do not disclose or disclose too late. The new Member States in particular have very detailed disclosure requirements for all Holders of Public Office, including legislators. There are bans on honoraria, limits on outside earned income, and restrictions on the acceptance of gifts. Another distinction concerns the time management of registers. Some countries require HPO and public officials not only to file financial reports, but also to file them within a given period of time. Majority of the countries surveyed provide an exact schedule of disclosure requirements, although the specifics vary. Polish legislators, for example, must file a financial disclosure statement within 30 days of taking office and annually thereafter. Similarly, in Germany, each Parliament Member must file a financial disclosure at the beginning of their four-year term, and they also must report any additional income, honoraria and gifts during that period. Some countries, such as the Czech Republic and Ireland, require that members file annually.

The popularity of public disclosure "seems due in part to the ease of implementation and the clear message it sends of a commitment to transparency in government."[162] In addition, obligations to declare personal interests in public will contribute to establishing a more open and transparent political sector, which is vital if legitimacy and citizen's trust is to be increased. However, a distinction should be made between public or confidential declarations of financial interests, the declaration of additional interests and whether declarations should be stored in a register of interest. Whereas in some cases HPOs and public officials

---

162 Gerard Carney, Conflict of interest, op. cit.

have obligations to declare only their financial interests, in most cases they must also declare other issues such as professional activities, honorary memberships and presentations in registers of interest. Thus the most important questions concern what should be declared, whether (or not) the declarations should be made public, whether (or not) independent bodies should have the power to monitor the registers and whether (or not) there should be sanctions for non-compliance[163].

Despite the popularity of these instruments, discussions on the pros and cons of registration obligation and obligation to register financial interests remain the subject of vivid discussions within the countries and the different institutions (see Table 8). One main criticism against declaration of interests in registers is that it should be designed for politicians and less for public officials. Next, the reporting systems are usually too simplistic, as they merely require a person to report in a very general way. An interesting illustration of this example is the comparison of financial declarations in the European Commission with those in the European Parliament. Whereas some Commissioners make relatively detailed declarations, almost all of the MEPs make very general statements in their forms (or simply reply "Nothing to declare"). This case illustrates that declarations and registers work only if requirements (as to what must be declared) are clear and known. Secondly, there must be a means to monitor these declarations and registers effectively and independently. Thirdly, there must be credible sanctions for non-compliance. If all of this does not exist, it will be difficult to detect wrong, misleading or partial information. On the other hand, financial disclosure policies and registers must be designed in such a way that the collection, storage and management of detailed financial disclosure forms will not cause a new conflict of interest bureaucracy. For example, the European Commission warns that "As far as the civil servants are concerned, the rules relating to conflict of interests are very clearly stated in the Staff Regulations. Introduction of a declaration of interests would cause important bureaucratic workload in

---

163 Hans Herbert von Arnim, Der gekaufte Abgeordnete – Nebeneinkünfte und Korruptionsproblematik, in: Neue Zeitschrift für Verwaltungsrecht, No. 3/2006 p. 249; Christian Waldhoff, Das missverstandene Mandat: Verfassungsrechtliche Maßstäbe zur Normierung der erweiterten Offenbarungspflichten der Abgeordneten des Deutschen Bundestages, in: Zeitschrift für Parlamentsfragen, No. 2/2006, p. 251; S. Muhle (2006), Mehr Transparenz bei Nebeneinkünften von Abgeordneten? Zur Weiterentwicklung des Abgeordnetenrechts in Niedersachsen, in: Zeitschrift für Parlamentsfragen, No. 2/2006, p. 266; Anne Käßner, Nebentätigkeiten und Nebeneinkünfte der Mitglieder des Deutschen Bundestages, Duncker und Humblot, Berlin, 2010.

terms of management, update, protection of data and there is no additional guarantee for a better fight against conflict of interests".

Table 8. Arguments in favour and against the use of public disclosure policies

Pro register, public disclosure and against professional activities	Against disclosure, public disclosure and in favour of professional activities
Legislators and Public Officials should serve the public interest and not the private interest Generally, pay is structured in a way that legislators and public officials do not need another job Additional professional activities would require too much time Additional activities influence the work. Consequently, private activities constitute a challenge to the need to act in the public interest The constituency has a right to know what legislators and public officials are doing, how much money they receive and from whom Public disclosure is the best way to control and to deter legislators and public officials. It is also a means of monitoring whether they use their mandate and position for the public and not the private cause Citizens have a right to know whether political decisions are the outcome of economic and private interests Additional and professional interests necessarily produce conflicts of interest In order to be in the position to	Legislators are not civil servants (and should never be) and should be allowed to exercise additional activities Too detailed public disclosure requirements violate fundament rights (right to privacy, right to exercise a profession, etc.) Experience shows that registers are not very functional. Often, the public is not interested in the registers. However, registers are abused by the media The introduction and monitoring of registers creates unnecessary bureaucracy Public disclosure does not reduce conflicts of interest Additional activities do not necessarily create conflicts of interests Additional activities allow for legislators to keep contact with "reality" (and with former jobs) Legislators do not need to work full-time Disclosure requirements can have negative effects as regards jobs that require a certain confidentiality (advocates, etc.) Too much transparency can harm individual freedom Voters should best judge and scrutinise the behaviour of legislators – and not

judge the performance of a legislator and public official people have the right to know what kind of potential conflicts of interest exist Transparency and openness are important elements of a democracy Self-regulation does not work in many instances. Thus, control is necessary	registers

Another problem is the legal challenge: whereas in some countries politicians are required to declare detailed information (e.g., also the income and assets of their family) in a register, in other countries detailed requirements to register are not easily accepted. For example, some countries believe that registers are in conflict with fundamental rights (rights to privacy, personal rights, family rights, etc.). Because of the different attitudes towards registers and financial declarations, some Member States require very detailed disclosure requirements, whereas others ask for much less information.

In Germany, the question of whether public registers are allowed and whether declarations should include detailed financial information was even the subject of a legal case in the German Constitutional Court (Bundesverfassungsgericht) in 2007. In fact, the Court turned down the lawsuit of nine German Members of Parliament against the German Parliament's Register of Financial Interest. The lawsuit aimed at a new code of the Bundestag, which obliged Members of Parliament to notify the Parliament President of their incomes and those of their family to their mandate. The ruling paved the way for a new code (which is, again, being amended).

4.3.2 Establishment of specialised ethics bodies, institutions, ethics commissions and advisory bodies in the field of ethics

4.3.2.1 Specialised bodies in the field of conflicts of interests

The development of disclosure policies raises the questions as to who monitors, supervises and controls the amount of information. This question is closely linked to the question whether and how the Member States monitor ethics policies as such. And who does it? A dependent body? An independent body? A ministry, agency, or a coordinating body? Another question is whether the

Member States have specialized committees or bodies that manage the implementation of ethics policies.

Principles of ethics cast suspicion on any process in which Holders of Public Office and public officials discipline themselves. "No one should be the judge in his own cause"[164]. This maxim has been guiding judges of controversies and makers of constitutions since ancient times. It expresses fundamental values of due process and limited government, providing a foundation for the separation of powers, judicial review, etc[165]. Consequently, most other professions and most other institutions have come to appreciate that self-regulation of ethics is not adequate and have accepted at least a modest measure of outside discipline.

Especially in the case of politicians and, even more, parliamentarians, independent and external control is rare. Mostly, the different institutions control themselves – if at all. This current practice is not satisfying since only outside and independent bodies are able to oversee and to monitor ethics rules and standards in a fair and impartial way. Outside bodies would also "be likely to reach more objective, independent judgments. They could more credibly protect the Members' rights and enforce institutional obligations without regard to political or personal loyalties. They would provide more effective accountability and help restore the confidence of the public in the ethics process. An additional advantage that should appeal to all Members: an outside body would reduce the time that any Member would have to spend on the chores of ethics regulation."[166]

Finally, the "move toward a more external form of ethics regulation is designed to enhance public trust and confidence"[167]. However, especially Holders of Public Office are very reluctant to accept independent experts to judge their Conflicts of Interest. This does not mean that the Member States and the different institutions are not willing to establish any form of control. In fact, Member States often agree on the above-mentioned forms of institutional self-control and establish internal reporting obligations and monitoring mechanisms. Despite current practice, the development seems to be towards the establishment of more external committees.

---

164 Dennis F. Thompson, Overcoming the conflict of interest in congressional ethics. Paper for the panel on Congressional Ethics Enforcement, Woodrow Wilson International Center, Washington, D.C., January 16, 2007, p. 2.

165 Ibid.

166 Ibid., p. 18.

167 Saint-Martin, Path-dependency, in: Saint-Martin/Thompson, op. cit., p. 6.

Table 9. Main differences between self-regulation and independent forms of ethics committees for Holders of Public Office

Self-regulation committees	Independent ethics committees
Members are internal experts, officials or elected/nominated HPO	Members are independent experts
Internal oversight. Committee Members oversee their peers' compliance with ethics rules	External oversight. Commission oversees compliance with ethics rules
Can be an office, Parliamentary Committee, Presidential office within own organisation	Independent with own budget, mostly controlled by Parliament
Duties can include: Advising colleagues on conflicts of interest Creating awareness for violations of rules of ethics	Duties can include: Providing ethics training Investigating ethics complaints own inquiry Determining penalties Issuing advisory opinions Receiving financial disclosure and monitoring reporting statements
Exist in most EU countries and in EU institutions	Pure models do not exist: US, Canada, Australia, to a lesser extent IE and UK

4.3.2.2 Structural features – powers, functions and resources of ethics committees on the governmental level

Unfortunately, little is known as to the functions and powers of ethics committees. From what is known, it seems that Member States provide for ethics bodies that give advice, but only few are allowed to investigate allegations and/or to impose sanctions. Other important differences include budgetary powers, and responsibilities for collecting and analysing private disclosure statements by the Members (or whether this is done by the personnel administration, the President, etc.). However, from a comparative point of view, very little is known as to the operation of these – relatively non-transparent – ethics committees, commissions, etc. Also little evidence exists as to their internal operations, budgets, rules of procedure and working styles. In the United States, the Congress and the Judiciary all have different ethics committees. In addition, thirty-six states have ethics commissions, which vary enormously in size and capacity. "Budgets vary from 5,000 dollars in Michigan to 7 million dollars in California"[168].

In Europe, the best known ethics committee is probably the Committee on Standards in Public Life and Privileges in the UK. In a survey by Saint-Martin the author shows that "Ethics commissions in the US are generally more powerful than in the Canadian provinces and in Britain. Their mandate is broader and covers thousands of government employees. And as a rule, they have the power to conduct investigations at their own instigation"[169]. Key differences between ethics commission in the US and those in Westminster concern the fact that the US commission covers officials in the executive branch, whereas most commissions in the Westminster system focus on the legislative branch. The main role of the British Committee on Standards and Privileges is investigating cases which have been recommended by the Parliamentary Commissioner for Standards. The Committee can also recommend penalties to be voted on by Parliament. According to Saint-Martin, the most powerful ethics commission is probably the Australian Independent Commission Against Corruption (ICAC)[170]. Its main function is to investigate allegations of unethical conduct by Members of Parliament, judges, ministers, police officers and all employees in government departments and local authorities.

Despite the fact that little is known as to ethics commissions and ethics committees in general, there seems to be a trend towards the introduction of more of these bodies. In most cases these committees are neither independent bodies nor do they have important monitoring and enforcement powers. Most institutions in the Member States of the EU are of the opinion that any form of self-regulation has the advantage that it is simpler, easier and less conflict-bound. Therefore, at least currently, the Member States and the European institutions prefer this model.

The problem with this practice is that the public increasingly tends to question practices where public institutions regulate their own ethical conduct. It seems to be the case that any form of self-regulation causes ever more suspicion. On the other hand, arguments against and in favour of the creation of an independent ethics watchdog are still more based on faith than on empirical evidence. There is also much confusion and exaggeration linked to independent watchdogs. In

---

168 Menzel, Ethics management for public administrators, op. cit., p. 135.

169 Denis Saint-Martin, Should the federal ethics counsellor become an independent officer of parliament?, in: Canadian Public Policy, Analyse de Politiques, Vol. XXiX, No. 2/2003, p. 202.

170 Ibid.

particular, the challenge facing legislative ethics committees is how to ensure their credibility with the press or the public. Most professions – including doctors, lawyers and teachers – discipline their own members through internal committees without facing accusations of attempts to protect their own. However, legislators who intend to discipline their fellow members face a higher level of scrutiny, one resulting from their commitment to public service.

4.3.2.3 Special units, institutions or bodies that investigate misconduct and corruption policies

As already mentioned, there is very little evidence as to organisational issues and the most effective institutionalization of ethics policies. Consequently, there is also no good practice case. Overall, the whole field of implementation and monitoring of ethics policies is hugely fragmented and opaque and also non-transparent. Moreover, differences exist as to centralized or decentralized bodies, finances, composition and powers of the different institutions.

In the field of conflicts of interests for Holders of Public Office, many Member States have established an internal body that oversees the conduct of the members of the institution. Depending on the institution in question these may take the form of a Parliamentary Committee or a specific Central Bank committee. In other cases the President of the Parliament is in charge of overseeing ethical standards. A model that depends on legislators investigating and sanctioning their fellow members can be problematic. Dennis F. Thompson notes that legislators "rarely report improprieties of their colleagues or even of the members of their colleagues' staffs, and they even more rarely criticise colleagues in public for neglecting their legislative duties."[171] Another institutional model involves establishing a regulatory system within the legislature or executive. Such a system is typically created through internal rules of procedures rather than through legislation. It generally takes the form of a Parliamentary committee composed of members, combined with an independent Parliamentary commissioner or commission. Ireland and the United Kingdom adopted this model in the wake of several ethics scandals in the mid-1990s. In the British House of Commons, members appoint a Parliamentary Commissioner for Standards who, along with the Registrar, maintains the Register of Members' Interests.

As regards the public servants, the existing structures are even more diverse. Still, it is possible to distinguish between specific independent bodies with investigative powers and other supervisory and monitoring bodies. In the Nether-

171 Denis F. Thompson, Political ethics and public office, Harvard, 1987, p. 108.

lands, the National Police Internal Investigations Department or 'Rijksrecherche' is the main investigative body. The Rijksrecherche is the only division of the Dutch police that falls under the exclusive responsibility and authority of the Board of Procurators General of the Public Prosecutions Department. Consequently, its role in the Dutch rule of law is moderate, but distinctive. Rijksrecherche investigations primarily focus on investigations against (semi) government officials (civil servants and elected/appointed officials) who are suspected of punishable acts (criminal offences), whereby the integrity of justice and/or that of the public administration (the government) is at issue. On the basis of its independent position towards the various police forces, the Rijksrecherche may also conduct investigations into the actions of police officers who in the performance of their duties used violence or were in default, as a result of which injuries occurred. The Rijksrecherche therefore contributes to the monitoring and upholding of an incorruptible government. Prosecutions remain the responsibility of the Public Prosecutions Department.

Also in Ireland, the Standards in Public Office Commission has power of investigation either on its own initiative or following a complaint. A Select Committee on Members' Interests can investigate a non-office holding member of the Oireachtas similarly. The Commission or a Select Committee cannot prosecute. Prosecution of an offence is a matter for the Director of Public Prosecutions (http://www.dpp.ie/). Where the Commission or the Select Committee, either during or at the conclusion of an investigation, is of the opinion that the person who is the subject of the investigation may have committed an offence relating to the performance of his or her official functions, it must prepare a report in relation to the matter and furnish it to the Director of Public Prosecutions. In the European Commission (the European Anti-Fraud Office and Investigation and Disciplinary Office), in Belgium (the Office central de répression de la corruption/police) and in Slovakia (the Anti-Corruption Office) the different authorities have also powers to investigate.

An intermediate case represents Malta and Luxemburg where the Public Service Commission, the Internal Audit and Investigations Department, the National Audit Office, the Permanent Commission against Corruption and the Commissioner of Police are bodies in place to investigate misconduct and corruption in the Public Service. In Luxemburg, only the Commissioner of the Police has the authority to prosecute, whereas Comité de prévention contre la corruption in the Ministry of Justice has not such an authority to prosecute. Contrary to the Netherlands, Ireland and Malta is the situation in a number of other countries where ethics bodies have a rather weak role. For example, in Spain, there are specific general inspection units in each department. However, these units do not have the authority to prosecute. Instead, they may inform the attorney about illegal conduct in the different departments. In the UK, the Expenses and Ethics Committee has no powers to prosecute. In the Czech Republic, there are no special bodies existing in the public service. Other Member States (like France, Germany or Finland) do not have specific investigative bodies within the public service.

4.3.2.4 Other institutions with tasks to coordinate and/or manage ethics policies

As regards the coordination and management of ethics policies, it is striking that most Member States have institutionalized only anti-corruption policies. For example, Portugal has established the Corruption Prevention Council (CPC). In the field of ethics, most Member States do not provide for institutionalised policies and there is no central coordination body on ethical issues in public administration. This may create a gap because of lack of an entity responsible for following up this issue both at internal and external levels.

Generally, it is possible to divide the Member States into two groups. The first group represents countries where specific ministries, bodies or institutions (or a combination of all of these) have been allocated responsibilities in the field of ethics policies. The second group is composed of countries which do not have (yet) specific ethics bodies (Denmark, Czech Republic, Italy, Germany and Finland). The first group consists of the Netherlands (Ministry of the Interior (and BIOS)), the European Commission (Unit HR.B.1- Ethics, Rights and Obligations and the Unit SG.B.4 - Public Service Deontology), Latvia (KNAB), Sweden (KRUS) and Belgium (le Bureau d'éthique et de déontologie administrative in the Ministry of Budget).

For example, in the Netherlands, the Minister of the Interior and Kingdom Relations (BZK) is responsible for the quality of the system, e.g. the laws and regulations. As such it has a coordinating role. As a result, the minister periodically monitors the extent to which the public administration has implemented an integrity policy according to law, regulations and policy. The minister has also monitored the integrity culture of public administration. Other important institutions are the National Integrity Office (BIOS), which is instituted by the Minister, and the National Court of Auditors (which has monitored the integrity policies of the Ministries and other agencies that fall under its jurisdiction). These organisations do not coordinate or manage the implementation process, but they play a distinctive role in stimulating such implementation. In the European Commission the leading body is the Unit HR.B.1- Ethics, Rights and Obligations and the Unit SG.B.4 - Public Service Deontology.

4.3.2.5 Conclusion

The institutionalization of ethics policies continues to become more complex and also more regulated in the Member States of the European Union. It is still highly fragmented and differs amongst the Member States. Generally, the Member States are much more active in the institutionalization of anti-corruption and conflicts of interest policies than in other ethics-related policies. As regards corruption and conflicts of interests policies, one can observe a trend towards the creation of specialized bodies to investigate conflicts of interest and corruption in the national public services. Ideally, these bodies should be independent. Still, only a few Member States provide for specific institutional structures in the field of ethics. Therefore, an ethics bureaucracy is mostly likely to emerge in the field of conflicts of interests as regards the management of disclosure policies, but less in other ethics-related policy fields.

At the moment there are more questions than answers concerning effective methods of ethics policies' institutionalisation. What are the experiences so far in monitoring and managing disclosure policies? Have the Member States ever evaluated whether the structures existing in the field of ethics (conflicts of interests, corruption and other ethics policies) are efficient and effective? Are certain coordinating bodies needed? Could advisory bodies, such as BIOS in the Netherlands, develop good practices and act as role models? What is the added value of specific ethics bodies? Should all ethics bodies enjoy institutional and financial autonomy? Alternatively, one could also ask another question: can the Member States still afford to have fragmented, weak or even not-existing organisational structures in the field of ethics? As we have seen earlier, one major obstacle and difficulty for an effective ethics policy is that ethics policies are not taken seriously. Is this reflected in the way how Member States institutionalize ethics policies?

5. PUBLIC MANAGEMENT REFORMS AND THE CHANGE OF WORKPLACE VALUES

5.1 Public management reforms, organisational justice and workplace ethics

Since the Northcote-Trevelyan report in 1854 in the UK, the merit principle has been considered a cornerstone of administrative life. Decisions should be taken as a result of fair and impartial procedures, according to the principle of individual merit and performance. In fact, for decades, conventional wisdom also assumed that organisational and personnel stability contribute to public administrative performance and impartiality. Originally, rigid careers and the seniority principle were invented in order to avoid patronage and in order to prevent political influence in the field of career development policies[172]. Also a lifetime tenure and high job security in the public sector was seen as an important stabilizing element.

In the meantime, most recent reform trends contrast with traditional thinking in the field of public administration. Already in 1996 the OECD identified the following eight forces[173] which still affect public service ethics and conduct:

- Working with limited resources as a consequence of downsizing trends, such as public sector freezing in many countries;
- Higher citizen demands or the pressures for more and better quality services;
- Restructuring the public sector or the trend towards the creation of autonomous agencies characterised by large managerial autonomy;
- A devolved and discretionary management environment or the trend to devolve managerial authority to individual managers;
- Public/private sector interface or increased contacts between the two sectors;
- Working in a fishbowl or greater transparency in government operations[174];

---

172 Matthias Pechstein, Das Laufbahnrecht in der Gesetzgebungskompetenz des Bundes, in: Siegfried Magiera/Karl-Peter Sommermann/Jacques Ziller (Eds.), Verwaltungswissenschaft und Verwaltungspraxis in nationaler und transnationaler Perspektive, Dunker und Humblot, Berlin, 2008, p. 673.

173 OECD, Ethics in the public service, current issues and practices, Public Management Occasional Papers, No. 14, 1996, pp. 17-25.

- Changing social norms or the increasing complexity and individualisation of society;
- Changing international environment or increased contacts of civil servants in different administrations with potentially different ethical standards.

With respect to human resource management, these trends correspond to changes in the field of employment conditions such as the move towards less job security and the flexibilisation of pay and promotion schemes. In terms of ethics, these changes can lead to different scenarios which also depend on the way these reforms are being implemented. As there is no direct causal link between these new trends in human resource management and unethical behaviour, it is perfectly possible in an initial scenario that civil servants stay loyal to or behave properly towards the organisation. But if we consider a second more critical scenario, we may also arrive at a slightly different conclusion. This approach highlights the unintended consequences of administrative reform on public employees. It starts from the assumption that reform strategies have an impact on the motivation, opportunity and possibility to act corruptly and that negative changes in the pay, promotion and discretion of civil servants can contribute to increasing uncertainty and alienation among employees, which can easily lead to disloyal and corrupt behaviour if the official in question has the opportunity to do so[175].

When looking from this perspective, one may wonder how issues such as flexibilisation, mobility and decentralisation have become quasi-sacrosanct principles, whereas classical principles and values like stability and centralisation are out of fashion. Also careers are seen as rigid structures which hamper mobility. In the modern literature, during the last years, only few experts have defended their usefulness. By contrast, nothing seemed more attractive than flexibility. This – at least partially – contrasts with the fact that the effects of organisational reforms are not without risks.

In the meantime, many Member States have also abolished hierarchical structures and careers, decentralized HR-responsibilities, outsourced many services and introduced business instruments. As regards the effects of these trends in the field of ethics, Frederickson has argued that corruption and unethical behaviour in government are on the rise because of attempts to run government organisa-

---

174 It can be argued that the increase in the number of cases related to unethical behaviour can partly be explained by the greater transparency and scrutiny.

175 Patrick von Maravic, Decentralised corruption in Germany, in: Public Administration Quarterly, Vol. 30, No. 3-4/2007, pp. 440-478.

tions as though they were businesses[176]. At the same time, Bovens and Hemerijck[177] concluded that the scandals that have attracted media exposure in recent years and given rise to public debate on integrity include activities and techniques that are relatively new in the public sector; specifically, privatization, introduction of market techniques, pay that conforms to the market, outsourcing of tasks and services, and commercial activities performed by civil servants or public agencies. Such issues all relate to the trend of introducing business- or market-like approaches into government. In one of the few existing empirical studies in the field, Kolthoff[178] concluded that new public management reforms may lead to less integrity violations. Rather to the contrary, they have positive effects on a number of integrity violations. Still, Kolthoff concludes that downsizing has a negative effect on integrity violations.

In this study we are interested in some concrete measures and their impact on ethical behaviour. For example, the decentralization of responsibilities, the reform of recruitment process, the reform of pay, job security and mobility policies. We asked the Member States and the European Commission whether certain reform trends are vulnerable to integrity violations. According to the results (see Table 10 on page 90), the most vulnerable HR reform trend to integrity violations are recruitment policies. Six Member States mentioned that recruitment policies are very vulnerable and 11 Member States stated that they are somewhat vulnerable to integrity violations. Next, pay reforms, promotion and mobility policies as well as austerity measures in general are also seen as having a negative impact on integrity.

---

176 George H. Frederickson, The spirit of public administration, San Francisco, Jossey-Bass, 1997.

177 Marc Bovens/Anton Hemerijck, Het verhaal van de moraal: Een empirisch onderzoek naar de sociale bedding van morele bindingen, Boom, 1996.

178 Emile Kolthoff, Ethics and new public management. Empirical research into the effects of businesslike government on ethics and integrity, Boom Juridische Uitgevers, 2007.

Table 10. Vulnerability of HR-reform trends to integrity violations (N=25)

	Very vulnerable	Somewhat vulnerable	Not vulnable	Cannot say	Total
recruitment policies	24 (6)	44 (11)	16 (4)	16 (4)	100 (25)
pay reforms	8 (2)	52 (13)	20 (5)	20 (5)	100 (25)
promotion policies	8 (2)	48 (12)	20 (5)	24 (6)	100 (25)
enhancing mobility between public and private sector	16 (4)	32 (8)	20 (5)	32 (8)	100 (25)
reform of job security	12 (3)	28 (7)	28 (7)	32 (8)	100 (25)
decentralisation of HR responsibilities	4 (1)	36 (9)	36 (9)	24 (6)	100 (25)
change of organisational culture	8 (2)	32 (8)	28 (7)	32 (8)	100 (25)
generally, the implementation of new austerity measures	8 (2)	38 (9)	13 (3)	42 (10)	100 (24)
organisational reforms (abolishment of hierarchies)	8 (2)	32 (8)	20 (5)	40 (10)	100 (25)
reforms of social security systems	12 (3)	20 (5)	28 (7)	40 (10)	100 (25)
openness	4 (1)	24 (6)	44 (11)	28 (7)	100 (25)
competency management	12 (3)	16 (4)	42 (8)	40 (10)	100 (25)
citizen-orientation	4 (1)	20 (5)	44 (11)	32 (8)	100 (25)
introduction of new ICT	0 (0)	17 (4)	63 (15)	21 (5)	100 (24)

Overall, one should be very careful when interpreting the data. For example, the figures do not tell whether reform policies lead to better or to worse results as compared to preceding periods. Second, most Member States have never evaluated the impact of reform policies on ethics. Third, the answers to this issue are official answers. We have no evidence about the opinions of employees, trade unions, etc. As a consequence, we have not enough hard evidence to say whether or not the introduction of new reform policies will lead to more integrity risks. Still, it is possible to say that some reform policies are likely to have an impact on integrity violations. From this, one may even go one step further: all the data indicate that the present reform trend in a number of areas (reform of recruitment policies, reform of pay systems, reform of mobility systems) are at high risk to raise more and new integrity violations. Therefore, we advise the Member States to carefully evaluate new reform measures and their impact on ethics and integrity.

5.2 Organisational reforms and decentralisation of HR policies

The ultimate measure of any HR system is the quality, efficiency, impartiality, professionalism and responsiveness that it delivers and how it furthers the possibilities to reach and fulfil objectives and helps delivering services of good quality to citizens. Basically, these objectives can be achieved by either a more classical or private sector like system, both of which have several benefits and risks, the advantages of one system often being the shortcomings of the other. Still, most current reforms in the public services of the EU Member States are dominated by moves away from the classical features of the bureaucratic model. In the meantime, almost all national civil services show features that depart from the classical bureaucratic model. Even more, some Member States have developed towards post-bureaucratic systems.

These trends away from the bureaucratic model include the flattening of hierarchies, flexibilisation of HR policies, introduction of enhanced mobility policies, reform and partial abolishment of careers in those countries with a career system, decentralisation of competences to regions and local administrations, decentralisation of responsibilities to individual ministries or agencies, delegation of responsibilities to managers, adoption of new accountability mechanisms and adoption of organisational and individual performance management schemes.
Most interesting is the question whether and how the decentralisation process affects the behaviour of employees. From a theoretical point of view, decentralisation undoubtedly has positive effects, but also poses severe challenges in the field of HRM[179].

Centralisation generally refers to the extent that decision-making powers are vested in bodies at a high hierarchical level. These central powers or rules are often applicable to the entire public administration. Centralised HR systems were put in place to guarantee politically neutral decision-making and to protect employees against political coercion and patronage. Moreover, it has often been argued that the standardisation of HR practices secures coherence of policies

---

179 Christoph Demmke/Gerhard Hammerschmid/Renate E. Meyer, Decentralisation and accountability as a focus of public administration modernisation: Challenges and consequences for human resource management, European Institute of Public Administration, Maastricht/Brussels, 2006.

and service delivery. In addition, centralised approaches are also seen to offer higher efficiency due to economies of scale and a higher effectiveness, because of qualified HR experts being in charge of tasks such as reviewing and ranking job candidates.

Proponents of decentralising responsibilities to managers assert that this increases the efficiency and effectiveness of HRM and public administration in general. Decisions can be taken faster, recruitment be tailored to the exact needs of the organisation, less complex procedures are needed, etc. In addition, effectiveness is increased, because decentralisation increases the manager's discretion, thus enabling him to recruit, evaluate, offer incentives, promote, suggest training needs and communicate directly. The philosophy behind decentralisation and deregulation is a well-known argument: centralised HRM is rigid, unresponsive, slow and ineffective. Finally, there is very little evidence so far whether decentralised HR systems are really more vulnerable to cases of political pressure and politicisation.

Still, highly decentralised systems may entail a decline in the professionalism of the core civil service and a certain loss of a civil service ethos, as well as the fragmentation of policies from a strategic point of view. In addition, the problem with such a decentralised approach is the increased possibility of conflicts among the different actors and institutions – ministries, agencies or HRM authorities – if central coordination mechanisms are ineffective or non-existent. The success of decentralisation also seems to depend on the skills of managers and HR professionals to carry out their tasks and responsibilities. Thus, greater autonomy and decentralisation of responsibilities require considerable investment in management qualifications at all levels. It is important to combine decentralisation efforts with additional management training to provide the professional skills that are crucial for managing in a decentralised environment. Fairness and equity are another important issue to be discussed. What happens when centralised procedures are removed regarding issues such as pay, promotion, diversity, equal opportunities? What happens if managers, different units, organisations and agencies apply their discretion too widely and in very different ways? Finally, decentralised HR systems may have unintended centralising effects if the HR functions are bundled and/or outsourced to one centralised entity[180]. Almost half of the Member States are also of the opinion that the decen-

---

180 J. D. Coggburn, The benefits of human resource centralization: Insights from a survey of human resource directors in a decentralized state, in: Public Administration Review, Vol. 65, No. 4/2005, pp. 424-435.

tralisation of HR responsibilities bears new ethical challenges (see Table 10 on page 90).

The reason behind is the risk that decentralised structures are more vulnerable to corruption[181] and issues of procedural injustice. Also new public management reforms lead to a decentralized organisational structure, empowered managers and less hierarchical control and supervision. The introduction of market mechanisms and competition increases the interaction with the private and non-profit actors and blurs the boundary between the public and the private sphere. Public managers have become more exposed to conflicts of interest than before. Therefore, decentralisation goes along with the need for additional co-ordination and new accountability procedures. Consequently, the effectiveness of decentralised systems depends on the existence of very good coordination and monitoring systems. Furthermore, specific forms of deregulation to 'let managers manage' can be accompanied by re-regulation that imposes new, and perhaps more burdensome constraints and additional bureaucracy. Sometimes, these are in the style of market-type mechanisms aimed at improving coordination or reliance on self-regulation within new frameworks of accountability and transparency such as performance indicators. However, these often appear to be no less intrusive or bothersome to managers than old-style by-the-book controls and inspections.

5.3 Impact of the financial crisis on workplace behaviour

Already in the 18th century Immanuel Kant concluded that nothing causes more indignation than injustice. Today, the OECD reports increasing levels of inequality in the OECD world[182]. However, this does not necessarily suggest that injustice also means that unfair treatment is also on the rise. All depends on how the principle of fairness is used. People are naturally attentive to the justice of events and situations in their everyday lives across a variety of contexts. Individuals react to actions and decisions made by organisations every day[183]. Unjust and unfair treatment can strongly influence the individual behaviour and

---

181 Patrick Maravic/Christoph Reichard, New public management and corruption: IPMN dialogue and analysis, International Public Management Review, Vol. 4, No. 1/2003, pp. 84-129; Patrick Maravic, Public management reform and corruption – conceptualizing the unintended consequences, in: Administratie si Management Public, No. 8/2007.

182 OECD, Government at a glance, op. cit.

183 Mark J. Martinko/Michael Gundlach/Scott Douglas, Towards an integrative theory of counterproductive workplace behavior: A casual reasoning perspective, in: International Journal of Selection and Assessment, No. 1-2/2002, pp. 36-50.

may exert a good or bad impact on individual and organisational performance[184]. With the coming of the financial crisis, ongoing restructuring processes are taking place in many economies on a global scale. Voluntary and involuntary redundancy, reform of (soft) retirement schemes, workplace transfers and the reduction of salaries do not only affect public sector and public service employees, but also have an impact on workplace ethics. For example, in the European Union, most public employees have seen their salaries and social benefits being reduced. Furthermore, recruitments are frozen and promotions stopped. How does this affect the ethical behaviour of these people? So far, there is also very little evidence on the impact of the financial crisis on workplace behaviour as such. Measuring the relationship between austerity measures and workplace behaviour is difficult.

From what is known, compensation and benefit reductions and adjusted work schedules, which have a direct impact on an employee's personal finances, life, and livelihood, are most likely linked to increases in misconduct, disengagement and less work commitment. Cost-cutting reforms are also linked to reduced rates of employee commitment and disengagement, which has been linked to employee performance and engagement. Overall, economic pressures, budgetary cuts, the reduction in salaries and promotion opportunities may result in more stress, competition and a general decline in organisational culture (ethical climate). In these situations issues such as fairness, courtesy, abuse of power and impartiality may be at risk. This again can result in more ethical violations, such as stealing organisational resources, misconduct at work, unwelcome behaviour, etc. Moreover, job satisfaction and organisational commitment is found to be negatively associated with overall perceptions of organisational and procedural injustice (for example in the case of injustice unprofessional performance assessments and unfair recruitment decisions).

In the European Union, the financial crisis has also supported speedier reforms of the traditional employment status (life time tenure, full time employment) under the so-called flexicurity agenda. As a consequence, more European states are confronted with growing inconsistencies as regards the employment of public employees in civil service positions. For example, more Member States employ a growing number of fixed-term employees in positions which should normally be offered only to civil servants with unlimited contracts. This has led to the fact that several Member States apply different employment relationships in

---

184 A. de Schrijver/K. Delbeke/J. Maesschalck/S. Pleysier, Fairness perceptions and organisational misbehaviour: An empirical study, The American Review of Public Administration, Vol. 40, No. 6/2010, pp. 691-703.

the same sectors, sometimes for the same professions and for employees who are working in the same office. Here, little is known on the fairness perceptions and ethical behaviour of civil servants, public employees and employees under short-term contracts. Do the different categories of staff show different behaviour patterns because of different employment statuses?

However, the financial crisis may also have positive effects or no effect at all on public-service ethics. It is even possible that during hard times, when an organisation's well-being or even existence may be at risk, the management talks more about the importance of high standards in order to guide the organisation through the crisis. It may also be that some are less inclined to commit misconduct when management is on high alert. In this study Member States were asked whether reform policies which are introduced as a reaction to the financial crisis have effects on workplace behaviour. As regards this question one should obviously distinguish between those Member States which have not introduced austerity measures (yet), and those who have done so. For example, countries like Sweden, Luxemburg or Germany have not implemented austerity measures[185]. For instance, Sweden informs that it "has chosen not to worsen working conditions due to the crisis. Nor has structural change increased this time, since government finances are in order and there is little need to cut cost for monetary reasons". Bulgaria, Czech Republic, Estonia, Greece, Hungary[186], Ireland, Latvia, Lithuania, Portugal, Romania, Slovenia, Spain and United Kingdom have implemented very tough austerity measures. Other countries like Austria, the Netherlands, the Slovak Republic and Poland are more difficult to classify, and for practical reasons we have classified these Member States as non-austerity countries.

Still, some countries replied "hard to say", because they had not introduced austerity measures or they did not have any empirical evidence as regards the relationship between austerity measures and workplace behaviour. The Netherlands replied: "Overall we have no cause for concern, although there is some debate on possible temporary effects on job satisfaction. We would like to point out that the effects might vary from organisation to organisation as a result of variations in the quality of management and the strength of the ethical culture". On the other hand, change is always going on and every year some thousands of staff

---

185 In this study we are focusing on austerity measures that directly affect individual workplace behaviour, such as the reduction of salaries and relaxation of job security. To our knowledge, these three countries have also implemented austerity measures but not as regards the reduction of salaries and easing of job security.

186 Consequently, the answer to this study from Hungary states clearly that there seems to be an increased fear for losing one's job.

are made redundant for structural reasons. A job security system, agreed between the social partners, supports noticed staff to find new jobs on the labour market.

Table 11. Impact of austerity measures at workplace level (N=25)

	Very much	Some-what	Not at all	Hard to say	Total
decrease of trust in organisation	8 (2)	36 (9)	20 (5)	36 (9)	100 (25)
decrease of trust in leadership	12 (3)	46 (12)	15 (4)	27 (7)	100 (26)
perception of unfairness compared to how private sector employees are dealt with	8 (2)	27 (7)	35 (9)	31 (8)	100 (26)
perception of unfairness compared to how colleagues are dealt with	4 (1)	35 (9)	27 (7)	35 (9)	100 (26)
decrease in workplace commitment	8 (2)	39 (10)	19 (5)	35 (9)	100 (26)
decline of ethical values	0 (0)	27 (7)	35 (9)	39 (10)	100 (26)
lowering of job satisfaction	27 (7)	31 (8)	15 (4)	27 (7)	100 (26)
increase in inappropriate use of resources, e.g., theft and fraud	0 (0)	4 (1)	48 (12)	48 (12)	100 (25)
unethical behaviour arising from higher stress levels and higher job intensity	0 (0)	4 (1)	46 (12)	50 (13)	100 (26)
increase in anger	0 (0)	46 (12)	19 (5)	35 (9)	100 (26)
decrease in loyalty	4 (1)	35 (9)	23 (6)	39 (10)	100 (26)
greater tendency towards corruption	4 (1)	12 (3)	46 (12)	39 (10)	100 (26)

The results of this study show a strong relationship between the introduction of austerity measures and workplace behaviour. For example, the impact of austerity measures is believed to be strongest in the field of lowering of job satisfaction. As Table 12 below shows, 83% of countries that have implemented austerity measures report lowering of job satisfaction. Austerity measures will also decrease of trust in leadership. 84% of austerity countries reported that the introduction of austerity measures leads to distrust in leadership.

Table 12. Lowering of job satisfaction by austerity measures (N=26)

	Very much	Somewhat	Not at all	Hard to say
No austerity measures	7 (1)	29 (4)	21 (3)	43 (6)
Austerity measures	50 (6)	33 (4)	8 (1)	8 (1)
Total	27 (7)	31 (8)	15 (4)	17 (7)

Moreover, many Member States report a decrease in workplace commitment. As regards the austerity countries, 58% reported a decrease in workplace commitment compared to 36% of the non-austerity countries. 73% of the austerity countries observe a decrease of trust in the organisation compared to 21% of the non-austerity countries. Also the degree of loyalty is influenced by the introduction of austerity measures. Whereas 58% of all austerity measures mention that loyalty levels are somewhat decreasing, only 14% of the non-austerity countries say that this is the case.

Table 13. Decrease in workplace commitment by austerity measures (N=26)

	Very much	Somewhat	Not at all	Hard to say
No austerity measures	7 (1)	29 (4)	29 (4)	36 (5)
Austerity measures	8 (1)	50 (6)	8 (1)	33 (4)
Total	8 (2)	39 (10)	19 (5)	35 (9)

Next, a relatively high number of answers report that public employees perceive increased unfairness compared to how colleagues in the public or in the private sector are dealt with. Interestingly, there seems to be no correlation between the introduction of austerity measures and the decline of ethical values as well as between austerity measures and unethical behaviour arising from higher stress levels and higher job intensity. As regards the latter, one explanation may be that causes for higher stress levels and job intensity can be found in many more factors than only in the introduction of austerity measures. Overall, the answers of the Member States reveal some worrying trends that should give reason to investigate the link between the introduction of austerity measures and ethics.

5.4 Reforming job security

Writers on public administration have long suggested that without a specific status, legal protection, lifetime tenure and special ethical rules, our societies would be open to terrible corruption (furchtbarer Korruption – Weber), and this would undermine the capacity of the state to rule society. Consequently, in 2003, the French Conseil d'Etat came to the following conclusion: "....the main objectives of the successive statutes of 1946, 1959 and 1983, were to establish in France an ethical, competent and non-politicised civil service, that is to say a civil service loyal towards the public authority, and which is protected from political and partisan pressures. This result is without doubt to be regarded as successful…"[187]. Consequently, civil servants' job security is still largely higher than in the private sector[188].

Table 14. Civil servants' job security compared to private sector job security by type of civil service structure[189]

(Frequencies in parenthesis)

		Differs	Does not differ	Total
Type of civil service structure	Career structure	89 (16)	11 (2)	100 (18)
	Non-career structure	56 (5)	44 (4)	100 (9)
	Total	78 (21)	22 (6)	100 (27)

From the point of view of the civil servants and the trade unions, the criterion of security is important especially in times of economic crisis. Another aspect of public service employment is the function of job security as a motivational instrument. In most Member States, job security in the public sector is an important motivational element for the recruitment and the retention of staff. At present, therefore, most Member States still agree with this argument that job security is important, but also argue that more job security can only be justified for specific positions and functions. Consequently, job security seems to be widely accepted as an important motivational factor. This is also in line with many studies that show the detrimental effects of job insecurity[190]. In this way, it is striking that almost one third of all Member States allow for the dismissal of civil servants in times of economic difficulties.

187 Council of State, Public report of the Council of State, Studies and documents, reflections on the civil service, Paris, 2003.

188 According to the data, only in Hungary, Poland, the Czech Republic, Denmark, Slovakia and Sweden civil servants' job security does not differ significantly from the private sector job security.

189 Christoph Demmke/Timo Moilanen, Civil services in the EU of 27, op. cit.

190 Bert Klandermans/Tinka van Vuuren, Job insecurity: Introduction, in: European Journal of Work and Organisational Psychology, Vol. 8, 1999, pp. 145-153; Hans de Witte, Job insecurity and psychological well-being: Review of the literature and exploration of some unresolved issues, in: European Journal of Work and Organisational Psychology, Vol. 8, 1999, pp. 155-177; Jonny Hellgren/Markus Sverke/Kerstin Isaksson, A two-dimensional approach to job insecurity: Consequences for employees attitudes and well-being, in: European Journal of Work and Organisational Psychology, Vol. 8, 1999, pp. 179-195; see also the case studies on Finland and the Netherlands.

The attractiveness of the public sector as an employer is also closely linked to the security of the workplace. In recent years many EU Member States have faced increasing recruitment problems, though the current slowdown in the economy is leading to an improvement in the situation. This, however, supports a false image of the public sector, since the number of jobs in it will be cut over the next few years. In the past, new recruitment only took place in a very limited way and because of this, the public sector has felt little incentive to present itself as an attractive employer. In the future, almost all European countries are expected to face recruitment problems in the fields of social services, IT and education. Yet, lifetime employment seems to be less important than it was some decades ago. As we can see, many Member States are moving away from the classical lifetime tenure principle. In more countries it is now possible to dismiss civil servants for various reasons (and mostly in cases of poor performance).

Furthermore, in some Member States governments pursue policies of reducing public employment and many EU countries allow for downsizing policies in the civil services. These developments show that it would be misleading to speak in a general way about the stability of public service employment. In fact, it is also true that people often have a false image of employment in the public sector since they believe that public employment is more stable than employment in the private sector. In fact, the issue of job security is still surrounded by many myths. For example, whereas people believe that all public employees enjoy lifetime tenure and greater job security, this is not always the case. In most Member States, public employees can be dismissed for many (mostly theoretical) reasons.

Today, almost all Member States maintain a system in which civil servants are enjoying a very high or a high degree of job security. In countries such as Germany or Ireland, lifetime tenure is seen as protecting the independence of civil servants, particularly given the requirement that they are able to give unbiased advice to the Government of the day. Civil servants are also expected to exercise high ethical standards of fairness in the discharge of their duties without bias, i.e. in relation to enforcement of regulations. Thus the instrument of job security is seen as important in protecting the civil servant against political pressure. Therefore, job security is mostly higher for civil servants than for other public and private sector employees. For example, in Denmark, civil servants are entitled to a three years' pay if they are dismissed due to abolition of positions.

Here, one may distinguish between countries with lifetime tenure (where dismissal is only possible as a result of disciplinary procedures), and systems with a high degree of job security (where it is possible to dismiss civil servants under specific conditions). In both cases dismissal of civil servants exists more in theory than in practice. Overall, 14 Member States still offer a lifetime tenure. According to data, career structure countries provide stronger job security than non-career countries. Mostly Eastern European countries (e.g. Slovakia) have relative weak job protections for civil servants. Countries with a bureaucratic career structure allow dismissals mainly for disciplinary reasons. In non-career countries civil servants' employment can be terminated for various reasons, for example for poor performance or due to economic difficulties.

In a comparative study, most Member States agreed that job security can be justified in order to protect employees from external pressure or political pressure[191]. On the other hand, the privileged treatment of public employees regarding job security and specific social security schemes seems to have caused frustrations in some Member States. Many people believe that public employees should not be treated differently to private employees. In addition, many believe that job security (or job tenure) will not enhance performance since public employees do not fear dismissal or sanctions in the event of poor performance. In the above-mentioned study Member States were also asked whether "The possibility of firing staff for poor performance may lead to higher performance levels, since staff would believe they are subject to sharper discipline". Most Member States did not agree with this hypothesis; only Denmark, the Netherlands, Lithuania, Cyprus and Italy were inclined to agree.

Most Member States stated that "dismissing people for poor performance is not a way to ensure higher performance", and dismissal is the last resort. The French contribution to the survey stated that it is difficult to improve employees' performance on the basis of fear of dismissal ("la crainte du licenciement"). The highest possible effectiveness should be sought via positive incentives, e.g., organisation of work, individual performance management, training, promotion, etc. With regard to this point, job guarantee is an important motivational factor which should be exploited dynamically.

In each of the EU-27 countries, civil servants' employment can be terminated due to disciplinary reasons. Countries such as Germany, Greece and Lithuania allow for the dismissal of civil servants only due to disciplinary reasons. In many countries poor performance also seems to be an adequate reason for ter-

---

191 The participating Member States agreed with the following statement: "The main argument in favour of lifetime tenure is that it compensates for the generally higher private sector salaries and, even more, enhances job protection for those employees with a regulatory or enforcement function and with jobs needing protection against individual and political pressure". Christoph Demmke, Are civil servants different because they are civil servants? European Institute of Public Administration, Maastricht, 2006.

mination. Restructuring, downsizing and reorganisation are reasons to terminate the relationship in more than half of the countries. However, despite the fact that these operations can analytically be distinguished from each other, it seems that in practice they measure the same thing and respondents find it difficult to differentiate between restructuring and downsizing. However, the general trend is towards a weakening of job protection for civil servants.

In the meantime, more countries also allow for other reasons such as poor performance and bad performance assessment to dismiss civil servants. However, in all of these countries it is still rare that civil servants are dismissed because of poor performance. The same is true for the Netherlands, Finland and Denmark. Although it is possible to dismiss civil servants in these countries for various reasons, in reality civil servants have a relatively strong (judicial) job protection. For example, in Sweden, job protection is managed relatively well, although lifetime tenure does not exist. For Swedish civil servants, there is a special job protection agreement that increases the already beneficial general conditions on the Swedish labour market. The aim, in case of redundancy, is to find a new job in the labour market as a whole, not only in the civil service. Even firing staff for bad performance is certainly not easy. Employers have to prove an employee's misconduct or deliberate misuse of power or resources. From the Swedish point of view, the possibility of firing staff for bad performance would have a disadvantageous side effect: the risk of losing trust between management and staff. Investments in enjoying work, encouraging confidence and promoting the common interest seem to be better ways of raising performance rather than strengthening discipline and stressing the internal formal execution of power.

However, the situation is different in many of the Central and Eastern European Member States which offer a relatively weak job protection. For example, in Bulgaria civil servants can also be dismissed when conflicts of interests arise. In Slovakia dismissals are possible in the case of loss of the civil servants' capability. When looking at these trends towards less job security, it is important to analyse whether these trends influence workplace behaviour, but also other issues, such as the degree of politicization. In fact, twelve Member States are of the opinion that the relaxation of job security is vulnerable to ethics violations (see Table 10 on page 90). Seven Member States have answered that this is not the case, as job security remains very high.

5.5 Effects of pay and social security reforms on ethics

Being forced to enhance efficiency in the national pay systems, many Member States have started important reforms of their pay systems. The objective is not always to cut salaries, but to completely reform the traditional pay systems and to link them with reforms of the social security systems. Another reason for the reform of pay systems stems from changes in perceptions of fairness. Whereas in the past, centralised and standardised systems were seen as fair (everybody received pay increases according to the principle of seniority), today people consider pay systems as fair if they are rewarded differently and according to merit and their individual performance levels. Both systems have their advantages and disadvantages.

In general, research illustrates that one can only attribute a limited significance to higher salaries in the fight against unethical behaviour, and more so when not combined with other measures[192]. Still, in their empirical analysis of the link between public sector salaries and the level of corruption, Rijckeghem and Weder[193] observed a negative impact of wages on corruption when public sector wages are relatively low compared to those in the private sector. Other studies, e.g. by Rauch and Evans[194], find no clear evidence of an impact of the salary level on corruption in the public sector.

In fact, our study clearly shows that some Member States are concerned about the impact of pay reforms and decreasing salaries on ethical behaviour in their national public services (see Table 10 on page 90). Indeed, salaries in some EU countries – compared to the salaries paid for comparable position in other Member States and in the private sector – are very low. In a number of these countries, poor salaries below the level of living wages lie at the heart of corruption. One may doubt whether public employees in Central and Eastern European countries can rely purely on the motivating power of the public ethos. What's more, "any suggestion that the personal rewards offered by the ethos should be seen as a compensation for low pay and poor working conditions for public servants should be rejected (...)the public service ethos should never be offered as an excuse for treating public service works less well than others"[195].

---

192 This statement is mainly based on Jens Chr. Andvig/Odd-Helge Fjeldstad (Eds.), Research on corruption: A policy oriented survey, Chr. Michelsen Institute (CMI) & Norwegian Institute of International Affairs (NUPI), Bergen/Oslo 2000, p. 108 onwards.

193 Caroline van Rijckhem/Beatrice Weder, Corruption and the rate of temptation: Do low wages in the civil service cause corruption, Working Paper WP 97/73, International Monetary Fund, Washington D.C. 1997.

194 James E Rauch/Peter B. Evans, Bureaucratic structure and bureaucratic performance in less developed countries, in: Journal of Public Economics, Vol. 75, No. 1/2000, pp. 49-71.

195 British House of Commons, The public service ethos, Seventh Report of the Public Administration Committee, 13 June 2002.

Moreover, countries like Ireland, Portugal, Greece, Latvia, Romania, Hungary, etc. have drastically reduced salary costs or costs for related issues such as allowances, bonuses, etc. How important is the salary factor? The above study by Rijckeghem and Weder arrives at the conclusion that fighting corruption on the basis of wage incentives could only be extremely costly to the authorities and that it would probably have only a limited impact if not combined with other instruments. So, they conclude that "if public sector wages were doubled, the corruption index of a country will be improved by the order of 2 points in the corruption index (CPI) of Transparency International". This of course means that very large salary increases would be needed to eliminate corruption.

Still, the question is not only to link pay reforms with corruption levels. Also important is the question whether pay reforms are related to perceptions of distributional injustice. Here, another question is whether the implementation of performance-related pay systems (PRP) is related to the feeling of being treated unfairly by superiors, and, against other colleagues. So far it is unknown how and whether all of these trends will affect ethics, corruption, conflicts of interest and politicization of public services. Even though concrete research results in this field are scarce and opinions differ, some publications provide the beginning of an answer.

However, people constantly compare their performance with the performance of their colleagues and mostly believe that they are better than others. In the case of standardised pay, many employees believe that their pay is not fair since they perform better than their colleagues. However, the problems are not solved once PRP is introduced and civil servants are paid according to performance. From now on, new feelings of being treated unfairly emerge and, in many instances, people are frustrated and even less motivated after the introduction of PRP. Since people constantly compare themselves with their colleagues, they also tend to believe that colleagues who receive bonuses and PRP do not deserve them. Employees who do not receive PRP are often becoming demotivated, since they expect to get bonuses. Another dilemma concerns the fact that many employees do not trust their superiors to take fair decisions on the allocation of PRP. Consequently, many people feel that they are treated unfairly because of unprofessional or unfair pay decisions of their superiors. In all of these cases, the expectation to be treated individually conflicts with the expectation to be treated equally. Thus, as long as traditional pay systems are maintained, they are seen as unfair and not corresponding to new value developments. However, the alternative may not be better. Demmke[196] suggests that returning to the traditional centralised and seniority-based pay schemes is not an option. Rather, it is important to design fairer pay systems under decentralised conditions. For this, one major challenge will also be to avoid discrimination in allocating bonuses and PRP.

In 2008, a study by the European Foundation for the Improvement of Living and Working Conditions revealed that "men are not only paid bonuses more often but the sums they are paid are also larger. Some 13% of male wage and salary earners had received at least €1,000 as a bonus for the previous year, whereas only 5% of women received such a bonus. A significant gender pay gap is also evident with respect to medium-sized bonuses of between €500 and €1,000"[197]. So far, only few empirical studies have analysed the pay gap between full-time employees and part-time employees, older versus younger employees, top-civil servants versus line managers and other employees, etc. In the future, the legitimacy of performance-related pay systems will very much depend on the question whether the bonuses are paid as a result of a non-discriminatory process. One may doubt whether this is the case today.

5.6 Mobility between public and private sectors

It would be unfair to suggest that people from the private sector are corrupt and immoral and that civil servants are moral. "It is perfectly possible, in the mixed economy of service provision, for an individual to take with them an ethos from one institution to another (...) whether in the public or private sector...The culture within the organisation is the crucial factor"[198]. However, it is clear that people coming from outside also bring other values with them. This can be interpreted both positively and negatively. Mostly, corruption appears in those cases where the person offering the bribe and the person accepting it have a close and long established personal relationship. As a consequence, the Member States concluded that by introducing more job rotation, the problem would be cured. Indeed, most governments are not only in a process of enhancing internal mobility, but are also bringing in more people from outside and offering them more fixed-term and short-term contracts. This development is important in order to bring different experience and fresh ideas from other areas. Nevertheless,

---

196 Christoph Demmke, Leistungsbezahlung in den Öffentlichen Diensten der EU-Staaten. Der moderne Staat, Vol. 2, No. 1/2009, pp. 53-73.

197 European Foundation for the Improvement of Living and Working Conditions, Effect of performance-related bonuses on gender pay gap, Dublin, 2008.

198 British House of Commons, The public service ethos, op. cit. p. 4.

these developments also bring another challenge. In fact, half of all Member States are of the opinion that enhancing mobility between the public and private sector is vulnerable to integrity violations (see Table 10 on page 90).

Therefore, for the future, it seems to be important to think about how the ethical values of the civil service can be maintained if mobility is increasing and appointments are made from administrations and sectors with different values. At least a minimum requirement would be to offer more training and offer induction courses on ethics. The dilemma is, of course, that if the Member States employ an increasing number of short-term employees and advisors, too heavy a burden would be placed on training budgets. Also, short-term recruitment should never be used as a way to evade recruitment through fair and open competition. Increased mobility into and out of the public service has a valuable role to play in the future, but it should not be an end in itself. From the point of view of public service values, mobility into the public service will be most valuable if it takes place within the setting of a vigorous public service culture sustained by a critical mass of professionals. However, one should also consider (much more than this was the case in the past) the link between values, organisational coherence and stability. Policies or systems that lead to excessive fragmentation, or to very different and short-term employment statuses, may not support strong public service values and a broad public service culture.

As regards the link between mobility and ethical standards, it would be wise to distinguish between different situations. For example:

- new appointees and recruits who are entering the public service from outside the public service (private sector);
- job rotation from other units, public authorities and/or departments within the public service;
- public officials leaving the public sector and moving to the private sector; and
- public officials going into retirement.

Specific ethical standards should be designed for all these cases. For example, public officials should be required to sign a declaration before leaving the public service to apply the duties of integrity and discretion with regard to facts and confidential information which have come to their knowledge while performing their duties. On the other hand, it is important to have provisions on ethical standards for former officials. In a number of Member States, former staff have taken over tasks as consultants. As regards this group of persons, it would be advisable to have clear rules on whether such persons are allowed to act as advisors or consultants for certain private firms. In this case, duties of discretion as regards the acceptance of certain appointments and professional confidentiality are at stake here. Compliance with rules on conflicts of interest should include provisions for former officials in new jobs never to handle cases of which they had knowledge in the course of their previous job. For example, in Austria, a new government bill is under discussion which will impose post-public employment restrictions on former federal civil service staff. They will be prohibited to work for a private sector entity (any entity which is not subject to the control of the Federal Court of Audit, a Court of Audit of the Länder, or a similar international body) for six months after leaving federal civil service. This only applies:

- if the decisions of the civil servant taken during the last 12 months of service prior to the resignation of his employment relationship with the federation (or his retirement) had significant impact on the legal position of the private sector entity he/she intends to work for; and
- if the exercise of the new job may harm trust of the general public in the objective performance of the former duties of the civil servant in question.

Additionally, as these restrictions are a constraint of the fundamental right to choose any occupation desired (as guaranteed by the Austrian constitution), these rules will not be applied:

- if their application may result in an in-equitable obstacle for the professional career of the civil servant; or
- if the last monthly salary of the civil servant has not exceeded a certain amount (linked to social security contributions, currently approx. 1.500 Euros); or
- if the federation in its capacity as an employer is responsible for the resignation of the civil servant.

In the case of a breach of these rules, the civil servant has to pay 300% of his last monthly salary (legal penalty).

As regards the recruitment of new officials or the timely nomination of senior officials from the private sector, it would be very helpful to train these people during the initial phase, and require every person to sign a Note on Ethical Codes and Standards of Integrity prior to taking up the job. It would also be worth considering including a similar statement in any personnel appraisal form in order to force officials to refresh their memory about ethical standards in their organisation. Similarly, officials in the financial sector should be aware of the national transposition measures as regards Council Directive 2003/6/EC on insider dealing[199] (such as making a profit on the sale of shares by using confidential and professional information).

Public employees, in particular, working in financial administration, tax administration, competition administration, etc., as well as their family members such as spouses, children and parents, should also be aware of any conflicts of interest that may arise in the case of holding company shares. As regards the latter, officials should also be required to fill in and sign a statement. In cases of conflicts of interest, the superior should be informed and act with the utmost discretion. As regards insider information, public officials should never advise other persons on the stock markets or other financial information which comes to their knowledge during their work.

5.7 Reform of recruitment procedures and their impact on ethics

European civil services have traditionally been closed systems. Civil servants were recruited for a clearly specified career path. Entry into these systems took normally place in at a level which was normally at the lowest end of the career. From here, civil servants would slowly move up in the hierarchy. The bureaucratic career system and the seniority principle allowed civil servants to move up steadily, but only from one grade to the next. Mid-career access to civil service functions was impossible, as was the recruitment of outsiders from the private sector into the civil service. This was to protect the administration from patronage and political influence. Classic civil services were built on the belief that civil servants remained in their positions for their whole life. They would neither move to other organisations nor leave the public sector to the private sector. Consequently, mobility policies did not exist, as this could lead to excessive politicisation of the civil services. Also, communication was highly formalised and followed hierarchical rules. Direct contacts with citizens and NGOs were highly unusual.

Although much of this looks old-fashioned in the eyes of the (post-) modern observer, there were good reasons for this. Public services should follow fair recruitment procedures. Posts should only be allocated according to objective criteria (e.g. merit, qualification, competence) and should not be subject to the influence of money, power, family ties or tradition. Thus, for a long time, the market was not seen as an alternative to public recruitment procedures. Walzer

199 Directive 2003/6/EC of 12 April 2003, OJ L 96/16.

explains the underlying reasons for this[200]: we do not like to expose people to public officials who are given jobs only because of personal reasons (and not because of merit and qualification). And we do not like to expose people to public officials who lack the necessary competence and qualification of the post in question. It would be unfair to allocate jobs to applicants as a result of non-transparent and corrupt practices. Thus, posts must be allocated to those who have succeeded in fair and neutral recruitment procedures, and who are qualified enough to carry out these posts. Consequently, impartial and neutral recruitment procedures should not be privatised.

For a long time recruitment procedures were also different from those in the private sector. Because of the specific duties and obligations of civil servants, they had to undergo a specific recruitment procedure. Traditionally, all Member States required candidates to pass specific concours, state exams and/or training if they wanted to be recruited as civil servants. Until today, this principle has not changed very much. Specific recruitment procedures still form an essential part of the bureaucratic career systems. As the results of the study by Demmke and Moilanen showed, almost all Member States still have specific, formalised recruitment requirements in place[201].

Despite the fact that almost all Member States still have specific recruitment procedures, all other traditional features in the field of recruitment are about to change. For example, careers are abolished, public servants can be recruited at any hierarchy levels, the mobility between public and private sectors is being enhanced (see previous subchapter), recruitment procedures are decentralized and flexibilised, etc. The reasons for this can be found not only in the change of values and the alignment of the public and private sectors in general. In fact, many Member States are forced to open up their civil services because of demographic changes, increased competition between the public and private sector and more mobility between the public and the private sector. Despite the anticipated positive effects of these measures, the reform of recruitment systems and their impact on ethics also have some unintended negative effects. Two thirds of all Member States expect that the reform of recruitment systems is vulnerable to integrity violations (cf. Table 10 on page 90).

---

200 We have used the German edition, Michael Walzer, Sphären der Gerechtigkeit, Ein Plädoyer für Pluralität und Gleichheit, Frankfurt/New York, 2006, p. 198.

201 Christoph Demmke/Timo Moilanen, Civil services in the EU of 27, Peter Lang, Frankfurt/M., 2010.

6. EXAMINING AND ANALYSING THE EFFECTIVENESS OF ETHICS INSTRUMENTS

6.1 Introduction: which human resource instruments should be used to foster ethics in the public sector?

In the past, tool boxes in the field of ethics were non-existent. The only instruments to foster ethics were legal rules, legal sanctions and disciplinary measures, the public service ethos and oaths. Today, the effectiveness of oaths is rarely discussed. In fact, oath can be an important instrument as long as it is used to raise ethical awareness and encourage employees to consider the importance of public service values. Oaths are widely used in almost all national public services. While some scholars believe that oaths have lost much of their value in the modern age and are seen as a formality or a silly symbolic feature of bureaucratic times, others perceive them as an important instrument. As Rohr noted, oath can be seen as a pledge to obey the constitution, but also as an initiation into a community of disciplined discourse, aimed at discovering, renewing, adapting, and applying the fundamental principles that support our public order. The task is to see the oath more as an act of civility than submission"[202].

Today, the Member States have a much wider arsenal of ethics instruments at their disposal than ever before. However, the effectiveness of the different ethics instruments has rarely been analysed. One of the rare examples is a study by van den Heuvel et al.[203] in the Dutch local municipalities, which came to the conclusion that rules for the declaration of costs are the most effective instrument followed by rules for the acceptance of gifts. The least effective instruments were rules on whistle-blowing, management plans and reports in the field of integrity and central registers for integrity violations.

Today, it is widely recognised that almost all HR policies – recruiting, evaluating, assessing, promoting, training, dismissing – have an ethical dimension. However, ethical HR policies should function in two ways. First, HR policies, processes and procedures must themselves be fair, professional and ethical. Secondly, it is the task of HR policies to make sure that only ethical employees will be recruited, promoted and supported. For example, recruitment should be carried out on the principle of fairness and merit. On the other hand, one part of the

---

202 John Rohr, To run a constitution, the legitimacy of the administrative state, University Press of Kansas, 1986, p. 192.

203 J.H.J. van den Heuvel/Leo Huberts/Zeger van der Wal/K. Steenburgen, Integriteit van het lokaal bestuur, op. cit., p. 74.

recruitment procedure or assessment should be to evaluate a job applicant for his/her integrity. Moreover, it is the task of any organisation to carry out highly professional and fair annual assessments, as evidence shows that subjective and unfair assessments will automatically produce perceptions of distributional or procedural unfairness. On the other hand, "putting an ethics component into human resources management is a daunting task, but one that many managers believe should be done. While challenging to incorporate an ethics criterion into evaluation, it would not be difficult to require employees to complete an ethics education or training course before being promoted"[204]. Another possibility is to include ethical components in an evaluation form.

What measures and instruments are favoured by the European states and the European Commission for encouraging proper behaviour on the part of civil servants? Is there an ethics policy and which instruments are considered to be the most effective? With respect to the different instruments, a certain consensus exists in Europe about the significance of the different instruments.

Most Member States believe that leadership is the most effective ethics instrument, followed by openness, laws and regulations and training (see Table 15). Furthermore, the answers indicate that the Member States prefer a mix of hard and soft measures. For example, laws and regulations are generally seen as important and effective instruments, too. The same is true as regards the need for effective training policies. It is interesting to note that many countries believe that post-employment rules are not among the most efficient instruments. In this context, it is important to note that many Member States are of the opinion that the regulation and management of post-employment is an issue of growing importance. However, the existing policies in place seem to be relatively ineffective.

204 Menzel, Ethics management for public administrators, op. cit., p. 80.

Table 15. Effectiveness of various ethics instruments

(1= effective, 5=ineffective)

	Mean	N	St dev.
Leadership	1.28	25	0.68
Openness, transparency	1.28	26	0.86
Laws and regulations	1.78	27	0.70
Training, incl. dilemma training	1.81	26	0.75
Codes	2.26	27	1.13
Protection of whistle-blowers	2.31	26	1.12
Registration of financial interests	2.41	27	0.93
Integrity officers providing counselling	2.46	26	1.07
Strict gift policies	2.67	27	0.78
Post-employment rules	2.93	27	1.11

Of course, there are other measures in the field of human resource management which promote integrity in the public sector by motivating civil servants in their work and with respect to their entire career. Key incentive instruments or instruments which may minimise the risk of unethical behaviour of staff in vulnerable positions include the following: fair selection and recruitment procedures, objective promotion criteria, opportunities for job rotation and enrichment, clear description of tasks, transparent division of responsibilities, separation of competencies, screening of staff, and sharing responsibilities among staff members.

6.2 Ethics rules – the case of disciplinary legislation

In general, the legal instruments governing ethical behaviour in the EU states are varied. The most traditional instruments aimed at combating wrongdoing and existing in nearly all states are penal codes and civil service laws, including disciplinary legislation. All Member States have some form of disciplinary legislation in place, with the main objectives thereof including the following:

- Ensuring that civil servants perform their tasks in accordance with the instructions received;
- Guaranteeing the protection of civil servants in a procedure subject to judicial supervision, including the right to be heard;
- Removing civil service status from civil servants who have damaged their public law relationship and have committed a breach of loyalty through a disciplinary fault.

The main differences concern the way in which disciplinary matters are dealt with. There are differences in the definition of inappropriate behaviour, possible sanctions or procedures called for. But there are also two distinct categories of countries in this respect: countries applying special disciplinary legislation to civil servants and countries where the disciplinary measures are not so much regulated in the form of law, but rather based on collective agreements or on rules similar to the conditions applied in the private sector. On the other hand, we can see that in countries where the disciplinary legislation differs from that in the private sector, civil servants generally have the right to appeal to specific administrative courts.

The most common sanctions are warnings, reprimands, changes and/or cuts in salary, forced changes of positions and dismissal. In many countries, breaches of integrity are subject both to penal law and disciplinary procedures. In general, a distinction can be made between strict and flexible systems, which is also evident from the definition of disciplinary breaches.

As noted above, legal, punitive instruments are necessary and important tools to combat wrongdoing. They set the minimum criteria for the professional and effective functioning of the public sector and establish clear procedures, mechanisms and sanctions for dealing with unethical behaviour, particularly with regard to serious cases of fraud and criminal activities. An ethical framework with a strong focus on punitive measures is best suited to highly formalised and regulated administrative systems which correspond to the so-called bureaucratic or Weberian model, and which are characterised by a rigid and narrow frame of action for individual civil servants. Often in these systems, there is less acceptance for codes of ethics with a more informal character, because they require strict observance of the rules and mechanisms of control for the fulfilment of the civil servant's obligations. This view is supported by the fact that codes of conduct are far more popular in Anglo-Saxon administrations (where they were introduced earlier) than in Germany, Luxembourg or Portugal, for example.

As regards traditional disciplinary law, the question can be raised as to what extent current disciplinary law is outdated or otherwise. This criticism was not so much related to the efficiency of systems or the legal protection of civil servants, but focused on the adverse understanding of ethics in this law. For instance, according to the authors, the traditional disciplinary system had been designed to be applied to public servants who had fewer responsibilities, who left all important decisions and actions to their political superiors and who worked in very hierarchical conditions within the administration. In this context, the question arises of whether a civil servant who takes on decision-making tasks in a modern administration should be subject to more active discipline and to professional ethics.

The question of whether to introduce more positive instruments, e.g. codes of conduct, in addition to the traditional legal framework is crucial with regard to a civil service which is increasingly moving from a rule-based approach towards a result-based management. Within this context of change – where the individual civil servant has far more responsibilities (the New Public Management literature refers to the empowered civil servant) – ethics is also becoming more complex. The relaxation of hierarchies and decentralisation also leads to more autonomy, increasing discretionary powers, and consequently to the need for better guidance and orientation, as well as for a greater awareness of what is ethically correct behaviour. Emotive questions in this respect are: is the current disciplinary legislation governing the behaviour of civil servants still sufficient to regulate the new managerial roles public officials are increasingly being required to play? To what extent is it possible to balance modern requirements of public management, e.g. aiming for results, targets and higher output, with basic ethical goals such as due process, loyalty and integrity?

6.3 Codes of ethics

In the field of ethics, rules and codes are still, by far, the most important instruments. During the last decade many countries have introduced numerous new rules and regulations to prevent unethical behaviour and to promote good behaviour. Today, a well-written and well-implemented ethics code is seen as a useful instrument that clarifies the values and standards of official behaviour. In the meantime, no administration can afford to have no code.

For analytical purposes it is useful to make a distinction between the code of ethics, code of conduct and code of rules and regulations[205]. The code of rules and regulations refers to legislative acts and other official regulations, setting clear behavioural expectations and disciplinary consequences. For example, in Finland, the Administrative Procedure Act defines the fundamental principles of good administration such as the legal principles of equal treatment and impartiality, and it regulates the conflict of interests (grounds of disqualification). It is important to notice that in some languages, such as German, the term code (der Kodex) cannot be used in the context of legislation, as code refers to informal

---

205 Montgomery van Wart, Codes of ethics as living documents, Public Integrity, Vol. 5 No. 4/2003, pp. 333-334.

guidelines without sanctions, so its usage matches with the code of conduct and the code of ethics.

Code of ethics, on the other hand, discusses the ethical principles of official behaviour. For example in the UK, the Committee on Standards in Public Life has defined Seven Principles of Public Life (selflessness, integrity, objectivity, accountability, openness, honesty, leadership) which apply to all aspects of public life. These principles are not statutory, but many public bodies have incorporated them into their internal standards such as codes of conduct. Codes of ethics are typically rather abstract and short documents (one to two pages). They are often used to announce fundamental principles, but they usually do not provide detailed rules nor advice on how to adopt these principles in practical situations. For example, most codes of ethics state that openness is one of the core values, but they do not provide guidelines on, for instance, how open civil servants can be towards the public on matters that are still under preparation. Unlike code of rules and regulations, code of ethics cannot be enforced, although some countries like Australia, Canada and New Zealand make adherence to the code of ethics a condition of employment which means that there can be consequences of varying degrees of severity for violation of the code. Sometimes codes of ethics are also called values statements[206].

A code of conduct lies in-between these two poles: it contains mid-level norms that set both aspirational values and expectation values. Therefore, their level of abstractness varies from moderately abstract to moderately concrete. A code of conduct can be seen as an extended code of ethics that transforms principles into practice. Most of the ethics codes used by professional associations are codes of conduct outlining not just general principles but detailed standards of behaviours. For example, see the American Political Science Association's code of conduct Guide to Professional Ethics in Political Science[207]. In Europe, a good example for a public-service code of conduct is the voluntary, non-legally binding Ethics Framework for the Public Sector[208]. It reflects the basic common values and standards which EU Member States consider important for the proper functioning of their public services. It comprehensively discusses the general core values, specific standards of conduct, actions to safeguard integrity and measures on handling situations where there has been a possible violation of eth-

---

206 John Raymond Boatright, Ethics and the conduct of business, Prentice Hall, 2008.

207 APSA, A guide to professional ethics in political science, American Political Science Association, second edition, revised 2008.

208 EUPAN, Main features of an ethics framework for the public sector, 2005; also published in Bossaert/Demmke, Main challenges in the field of ethics and integrity in the EU Member States, op. cit., pp. 253-267.

ics. The code of ethics is associated with the "high-road" or integrity-based ethics regime, while the code of rules and regulations is associated with the "low-road" or compliance-based ethics regime.

The distinctions made between code of ethics, code of conduct and code of rules and regulations is a heuristic device, but in practice these terms are often used interchangeably. A clear majority of the OECD and EU Member States have introduced codes of ethics and/or codes of conduct[209]. Although these tools are not mutually exclusive and can be used simultaneously, the code of conduct generally includes the core values, thus eliminating the need for a separate values statement. These tools can be used on many levels: there may be a general code of conduct, branch-specific codes of conduct and agency-specific codes of conduct. General codes apply to all public servants working in the central state administration, whereas branch-specific codes apply to officials working in a particular branch or sector of government, such as the judicial branch. Agency-specific codes apply only to the public officials of a particular organisation in question. Exactly what kind of ethics codes should be used depends on the legal, cultural and administrative context. If a country suffers from serious problems, such as corruption, then the code of rules and regulations is probably the right solution because it contains stronger deterrent tools to prevent misbehaviour (e.g. police investigates, court of law decides penalties). However, if the country wants to change its administrative culture towards more openness and better service, i.e. to create aspirational values, then the code of ethics or code of conduct should be given priority.

Still, the question remains open as to the effectiveness of these instruments. Especially codes of ethics and codes of conduct may take different forms. In addition, they differ as to the subjects dealt with. They are often suited to fight mild forms of misbehaviour and are in many ways a direct response to a dynamic and changing civil service environment which calls for clearer guidance. One of the main weaknesses of codes of ethics and codes of conduct is that in most cases they are characterized by weak enforcement mechanisms. This means that, on the one hand, they are more vulnerable to non-observance and violations, and, on the other hand, their successful implementation depends to a large extent on the existence of an environment of trust and an ability to ensure the organisational adherence to the code.

---

209 Moilanen & Salminen, Comparative study on the public-service ethics of the EU Member States, op. cit.; OECD, Trust in government, op. cit.

"The conventional wisdom is that codes have a positive influence in governance, especially in deterring unethical acts by ethically motivated public servants. That is, unethical officials are likely to be unethical regardless of whether a code exists, but those who want to be ethical find a code helpful in guiding their behaviour"[210]. The most important analysis on the effectiveness of codes has been written by Gilman. According to him, codes can only be successful as long as they have clear behaviour objectives. They should also fit into organisational mission plans and objectives. Next, codes should be modest and not promise what they cannot hold (ending corruption). "Most codes fail because they raise unrealistic expectations or they try to control too much. Codes that require excessive reporting and tracking can produce cynicism within the organisation and the public"[211].

Although these tools are not mutually exclusive and can be used simultaneously, the code of conduct generally includes the core values, thus eliminating the need for a separate values statement. These tools can be used on many levels: there may be a general code of conduct, branch-specific codes of conduct and agency-specific codes of conduct. General codes apply to all civil servants working in the central state administration, whereas branch-specific codes apply to civil servants working in a particular branch or sector of government, such as the judicial branch. Agency-specific codes apply only to the public officials of a particular organisation in question. What kind of ethics codes should be used depends on the legal, cultural and administrative context. If a country suffers from serious problems, such as corruption, then the code of rules and regulations is probably the right solution, because it contains stronger deterrent tools to prevent misbehaviour (e.g. police investigates, court of law decides penalties). However, if the country wants to change its administrative culture towards more openness and better service, i.e. to create aspirational values, then code of ethics or code of conduct should be considered.

The recent trend towards the adoption of more codes of ethics matches with recent public management reform trends towards the adoption of more informal and not legally binding instruments. Still, the question remains open as to the effectiveness of these instruments. Especially codes of ethics and codes of conduct may take different forms. In addition, they differ as to the subjects dealt with. Often, codes are suited to fight mild forms of misbehaviour and are in many ways a direct response to a dynamic and changing civil service environment, which calls for clearer guidance for civil servants. One of the main weak-

---

210 Ibid., p. 61.
211 Ibid., p. 69.

nesses of codes of ethics and codes of conduct is that in most cases, they are characterised by weak enforcement mechanisms as compared to codes of regulations. This means that, on the one hand, they are more vulnerable to non-observance and violations, and, on the other hand, their successful implementation depends to a large extent on the existence of an environment of trust and an ability to ensure the organisational adherence to a code.

In comparison to punitive measures, which in the event of non-compliance with ethical principles are characterised by sanctions, the main function of codes of conduct is to guide civil servants and to increase awareness in relation to the moral aspects of their tasks[212]. One of their major goals is to increase ethical sensitivity and judgement, and to provide clarity regarding responsibility. As compared to laws which are binding, a code of conduct is a much milder instrument to combat wrongdoings in the sense that it does not have such an imperative character and that it complements existing legislation and regulations. Bar Cendon describes codes of conduct as "provisions of a positive nature, which establish ethical principles, standards and guides for daily operation and stimulate the reward of good behaviour"[213]. They are mostly suited to fight mild forms of misbehaviour and are in many ways a direct response to a dynamic and changing civil service environment, which calls for clearer guidance for civil servants.

A further major difference between the EU Member States, Bulgaria and the European Commission is the level at which this code has been adopted, as well as the target group to which it refers. Most of the codes of conduct are drawn up by central government, while in some countries this competence is delegated to a decentralised or operational level. An example of organisational differentiation is, for instance, Sweden, where each public organisation may have its own code of conduct or ethical code, and therefore has the possibility to implement such a code.

---

212 On this topic, see for instance Alain Lawton, Developing and implementing codes of ethics, paper presented at the EGPA Annual Conference, Lisbon 3rd- 6th September 2003; Antonio Bar Cendon, Accountability and public administration: Concepts, dimension, developments, in: Michael Kelly (Ed.), Openness and transparency in governance, European Institute of Public Administration, Maastrict, 2000; Eleanor Glor, Codes of conduct and generations of public servants, in: International Review of Administrative Sciences, Vol. 67, London 2001, pp. 525-541; M. Maguire, Ethics in the public service - Current issues and practice, paper presented at the EGPA Annual Conference in Leuven in 1997.

213 Antonio Bar Cendon, op.cit., p. 65.

Table 16. Use of different types of ethics codes in EU Member States

(Frequencies in parenthesis)

	In use	Partly in use	Not in use	Total
General legislation	62 (16)	19 (5)	19 (5)	100 (26)
Code of conduct	59 (16)	7 (2)	33 (9)	100 (27)
Code of ethics	59 (16)	15 (4)	26 (7)	100 (27)
Specific ethics legislation	42 (12)	19 (5)	37 (10)	100 (27)

Table 16 confirms that different ethics codes are widely in use among the Member States. Based on the information gained from the data, almost two thirds of the countries use general legislation (62%), code of conduct (59%) and code of ethics (59%), followed by ethics-specific legislation (42%). In addition to these general ethics codes, virtually all countries have adopted agency-specific codes of conduct (88%) or field-specific codes of conduct (89%). For example, in the Netherlands, public organisations are obliged to adopt their own codes of conduct. In the European Commission some directorates-general have their own codes of conduct which take into account specific situations in DGs. Many countries, such as Cyprus and Slovenia, are using a specific code of conduct for the customs officials. Compared to the situation five years ago[214], it is evident that the codes are more diverse than before. However, it seems that some Member States are not able to distinguish between codes of conduct and codes of ethics, and thus use them interchangeably. Practically speaking general legislation and specific codes of conduct support each other, and likewise, detailed ethics legislation and abstract codes of ethics complement each other. Other combinations between them do not bring added value.

One of the main limitations of codes of conduct is that in most cases they are characterised by weak enforcement mechanisms as compared to other instruments. This means, on the one hand, that they are more vulnerable to non-observance and violations, and on the other hand, their successful implementation depends to a large extent on the existence of an environment of trust and being able to ensure the organisational adherence to a code.

The literature relating to this topic largely agrees on the conditions of how to encourage the setting up of codes which have the necessary authority to be respected by staff. A significant factor to consider is consultation with key stake-

---

214 Moilanen & Salminen, Comparative study on the public-service ethics of the EU Member States, op. cit.

holders in the development phase, or in a more general way, the involvement of staff or staff representations in the drafting of such a code. A further prerequisite for an effective code of conduct is that its content is expressed in such a way that it can easily be understood and implemented by the relevant target group. This hurdle can easily be overcome by drafting a code, which is clear, consistent, and comprehensive, and which has practical implications. Consistency means that it harmonises with existing legislation and procedures, while clarity should aim at minimising ambiguity[215].

Some research in this context goes even further and sees a link between the effectiveness of codes of ethics and generation-related factors[216]. The main arguments are that codes of conduct, in order to function well, must be adapted to the mentality of a generation and that substantial differences in values exist between the different generations. Consequently, there is a risk that existing codes are not convincing enough or do not have the required authority to guide civil servants in their behaviour. This may apply even more if the values contained in the codes of conduct are not supported by political and administrative leaders. For instance, the younger generations' beliefs are far more focused on individuality, innovation and economy, and not so much on authority, law and order.

Furthermore, the effectiveness of codes might be weakened if they do not reflect the organisational culture in an adequate way. In this context, it is not wise to copy codes from one organisation to another or to transpose a code without taking into account environmental factors. In the worst case scenario, this may lead to public officials being tempted to follow the example of others. even if such contradicts the formal guidelines, and to observe the content of the code only as a second step[217].

A further significant factor for guaranteeing an effective functioning of codes relates to the implementation phase. Quite often, drafting of codes of conduct is looked upon as being an end in itself. This is only the first step, and in order to make the code a viable document and part of the organisational culture, an appropriate way must be found of making the staff aware of the code.

---

215 Lawton, op.cit., p. 4.

216 Eleanor Glor, Codes of conduct and generations of public servants, op. cit.

217 C.L., Jurkiewicz, The phantom code of ethics vs. the formal code of ethics: The battle between right and wrong amidst a culture of reform. Paper delivered at the first specialised international conference of the IIAS, Sunningdale, UK, 12-15 July 1999, in: Antonio Bar Cendon (Ed.), Accountability in public administration: reconciling democracy, efficiency and ethics, Brussels, IIAS, 2000.

6.4 Leadership

Especially as regards values and raising awareness, the example of leaders' behavioural attitudes or values plays an equally important role as formal rules. Learning to uphold values happens mostly by way of example and role models. People learn to abide by values not through rules, but through parents, teachers, friends, colleagues and superiors. As regards public-service ethics, the quality of leadership is of paramount importance. If leaders employ the public values of loyalty, neutrality, impartiality and devotion in the democratic process, the chances are higher that others will do the same. On the other hand, one should not expect leadership only to come from the top. Other employees, too, have an equal obligation to educate themselves and their colleagues. Another important role of leadership is to demonstrate fundamental values and, in particular, to contribute to the spread of the civil service ethos. Moreover, leaders have a dual responsibility. They are not only a role model for others, but also the most important category of staff which is vulnerable to corruption and fraud.

Therefore, since leadership is so important, the Member States should do more to ensure that leaders can assume their responsibilities. Similar standards must be set for political leaders. If politicians do not observe the law themselves, it is hardly likely that they will have the authority to make others do so. In that regard, several scholars[218] consider good and ethical leadership to be a crucial factor in predicting and explaining integrity violations.

In the Dutch study[219] concerning the effectiveness of 21 anti-corruption strategies (see Table 6 on page 66), the key role was given to the administrative and political management. In this sense, 86.9% were of the opinion that more commitment by politicians is a key variable to combat unethical behaviour (internal control and supervision: 86.5%). It is also rather revealing – but also logical – that the variable "example given by management at the top" (80%) also scored relatively high. Leadership as a crucial instrument in fostering an ethical civil service was also supported by a study which was carried out in the Swiss federal

---

218 Michael E. Brown/Linda K. Trevino, Ethical leadership: A review and future directions, In: The Leadership Quarterly, Vol. 17, 2006, pp. 595-616; Karin Lasthuizen, Leading to integrity: Empirical research into the effects of leadership on ethics and integrity, Enschede, Printpartners Ipskamp, 2008; R. Cropanzano/F.O. Walumbwa, Moral leadership: A short primer on competing perspectives, in: Schmink (Ed.), Managerial ethics, pp. 21-53.

219 L.W.J.C Huberts, What can be done against public corruption and fraud, op. cit.

administration[220], according to which the most important factors for irregular behaviour are management mistakes, recruitment mistakes and poor organisation of competences[221].

There is substantial evidence that unethical behaviour is mostly an elitist problem related to leadership. In many countries those persons receiving bribes occupy leading positions[222], and almost all those offering bribes (87.1%) hold senior positions (owners of companies, directors, senior employees)[223]. In Australia employees who believed that they had experienced harassment or bullying in the last 12 months were asked who was responsible. Forty two percent named their supervisor, and 37% identified someone more senior other than their supervisor. In other words, nearly four out of five cases of perceived bullying and harassment involved managers. Even if we keep in mind that giving critical performance feedback or refusing to accede to unreasonable requests may be sometimes misinterpreted by some staff as bullying and harassment, it is still a worrying figure[224].

A further important question to be considered in this context is which type of leader encourages which type of behaviour? Needless to say, this is a difficult question to which there is no easy answer, particularly as there are a multitude of different leadership types and styles. Huberts[225], by referring to Badaracco and Ellsworth, distinguishes between political, directive and value-driven leadership. He arrives at the not very surprising conclusion that integrity in the public sector can only be encouraged by leaders with integrity, and by a leadership which is characterised by

- A consistent and coherent set of distinct objectives;
- A clear set of values;
- Correct behaviour;

---

220 Ethik im öffentlichen Dienst, Report of the Parliament's administrative supervisory authority for the attention of the Audit Committee of the National Council of 30 October 1998.

221 The relevant question in this respect was what the interviewees believed were the main causes of corruption and other breaches of CoI rules.

222 This figure applies to the situation in the private and public sector. Bundeskriminalamt, Lagebild Korruption, Bundesrepublik Deutschland, 30.6.2003, p. 32.

223 Ibid.

224 Lynelle Briggs, Testing APS Ethics, op. cit., pp. 119–136.

225 L.W.J.C Huberts/J.H.J. van den Heuvel (Eds.), Integrity at the public-private interface, Shaker, Maastricht, 1999, p. 18; Joseph L.Badaracco/Richard Ellsworth, Leadership and quest for integrity, Harvard Business School, Harvard, 1993.

- Charisma;
- Professional management.

None of these ideals seem to correspond to the requirements entirely, although the directive leader whose management style is characterised by a top-down approach with clear objectives, and the value-driven leader whose leadership is based on unambiguous moral principles, score higher. In comparison, the characteristics of the political leader, whose style is characterised by adaptation, negotiation and manipulation skills, is the least suited to leadership which encourages ethical behaviour on the part of civil servants.

Another survey by Karin Lasthuizen analyses the impact of the three following leadership styles and their relationship to specific forms of integrity violations: (1) role modelling by setting a good example to employees; (2) strictness in order to tackle employee misbehaviour; and (3) openness in order to discuss problems and dilemmas. The most interesting result of this study is that specific types of integrity violations demand specific leadership behaviour. In addition, the relationship between these three leadership features and specific integrity violations is demonstrated. In this respect, the main findings of this study can be summarised as follows: Firstly, the ideal type of leadership in the sense that effective curbing of unethical behaviour would be characterised by all three leadership characteristics. Secondly, role modelling is especially effective in dealing with unethical behaviour in interpersonal relationships. Thirdly, strictness is quite important in dealing with ethical questions regarding the misuse of organisational resources. Fourthly, openness is more important when role modelling and strictness have little or no influence on unethical behaviour. What is quite revealing with regard to the question of finding the right balance between a compliance-based approach and an integrity-based approach is that the significance of openness for curbing integrity violations is of lesser importance, while strictness and role modelling have approximately the same impact.

The quality of leadership is under pressure in many countries. Financial pressures, delegation of responsibilities, increasing complexity of the tasks, and contacts with the private sector mean that an increasing number of senior officials bear a heavy workload. Urgency and time pressures increase stress. Acting ethically and being a role model under these circumstances represents a big challenge. In our study 60% of the responding countries mentioned that trust in leadership is decreasing (see Table 11 on page 96). This represents a huge challenge for the Member States.

Even more, despite the fact that leadership is clearly seen as the most important instrument in the fight against corruption and unethical behaviour, the lack of leadership and leadership commitment is also seen as a major obstacle and difficulty for an effective ethics policy. Moreover, in the context of the management of the financial crisis, trust in leadership is decreasing in many countries. Thus, expectations and reality differ enormously.

The findings are interesting in many respects in the context of this study. The first conclusion is that there is an increasing gap between leadership expectations and the reality of ethical leadership. Second, due to the different correlation between integrity violations and management styles, the EU Member States and the European Commission would need different styles of leadership according to the dominant type of unethical behaviour. Consequently, states where unethical behaviour relates mainly to internal corruption such as favouritism/nepotism or poor treatment of colleagues or citizens (internal corruption, discrimination and sexual harassment), would need a leadership type that focuses on role modelling or setting a good example for employees. On the other hand, states with corruption such as fraud, theft, waste and abuse of organisational resources, abuse and manipulation of information, conflicts of interest through gifts, would require a stricter type of leadership. Third, the financial crisis has a negative impact on ethical leadership and trust in leadership. In reality, leadership represents a major obstacle and difficulty for an effective ethics policy.

6.5 Training

Ethics training is different than ethics education. Normative ethics theories, such as utilitarianism, principle or duty-based ethics, and virtue theory are unlikely to be touched upon in ethics training. Instead, typical ethics training consists of awareness rising for rules, codes and principles, dilemma-training, leadership training, conflicts of interest, etc. The steady growth in ethics training at all levels of government is prima facie evidence that is believed effective in discouraging unethical behaviour and encouraging ethical behaviour. Also our study confirms that the Member States consider ethics training as an effective instrument in the fight against corruption and unethical behaviour (see Table 15 on page 111).

Table 17. Communication of ethics rules through different types of training

	Frequency
part of in-house training	20
automatically provided when someone joins the public service	17
part of external training	15
automatically provided when someone takes a position in a different organisation	12
part of the employment contract/document	10
part of e-training	9

Out of the 27 received responses, three Member States claimed that in their country civil servants are very well aware of the ethics rules, eighteen said that they are well aware of the rules, while five countries said that the situation is difficult to describe. Since almost all Member States report that civil servants are very familiar or at least familiar with the existing public service values and standards, one could say that the ethics training is effective and reaches its goals. Overall, 20 Member States say that ethics is a part of in-house training, and in 15 Member States it is part of external training (categories are not mutually exclusive). In 17 cases ethics codes are automatically provided when somebody joins the public service. For example, in Spain ethics legislation and code of conduct for civil servants are part of the compulsory knowledge to become a civil servant. In Cyprus, persons appointed to the public service attend induction seminars which discuss, among other topics, the public service legislative and functional framework placing emphasis on the duties and responsibilities of public servants and ethical matters in general.

However, it is difficult to find definitive evidence whether training is really effective. There are few systematic studies of the effectiveness of ethics training in either the public or private sectors"[226]. A crucial component of ethics training is to make people ethically competent. What knowledge, skills and abilities does one need to be ethically competent? Menzel defines the following[227]:

- Be knowledgeable of ethical principles;
- Be aware and informed of relevant professional codes of ethics;
- Recognize and promote constitutional principles of equity, fairness, representativeness;
- Respect the law;

226 Menzel, Ethics management for public administrators, op. cit., p. 56.
227 Ibid., pp. 19-20.

- Serve the public interest;
- Engage in ethical reasoning;
- Be responsible for one´s behaviour;
- Guard against conflict of interest or its appearance;
- Respect and protect privileged information, etc.

Accordingly, any ethics training programme should include elements on issues such as:

- Highlighting the importance of values and code of conduct in the work place;
- Dilemma training and ethical issues involving challenging situations;
- Ethical decision-making;
- Ethical leadership;
- Criteria and other assessment tools for recruitment and promotion that test ethical awareness;
- Encouraging and assisting organisations to better integrate ethics into their management, incl. whistle blowing;
- Advice, guidance and training on harassment and bullying and the legitimate exercise of management responsibility;
- Courses on the fight against corruption and fraud.

6.6 Conclusions

Whilst there is a direct relationship between low salaries and unethical behaviour, increasing salaries will not necessarily reduce levels of unethical behaviour[228]. Higher salaries have a limited effect in the fight against unethical behaviour, and more so when not combined with other measures. However, one should not forget that many public officials in almost all Member States are very concerned about the impact of decreasing salaries and other social provisions. Poor salaries lie at the heart of corruption in many countries. One may doubt whether public employees in Central and South-Eastern European countries can rely purely on the motivating power of the public ethos. What is more, any suggestion that the personal rewards offered by the ethos should be seen as compensation for low pay and poor working conditions for public servants should be rejected. In addition, the public service ethos should never be offered as an excuse for treating public service workers less well than others[229].

---

228 Bossaert/Demmke, Main challenges in the field of ethics and integrity in the EU Member States, op. cit.

229 British House of Commons, The public service ethos, op. cit.

In addition to fair salaries, adequate training and good leadership, there are other measures in the field of human resource management which promote integrity in the public sector by motivating civil servants in their work and with respect to their entire career. Key incentive instruments or instruments which may minimise the risk of unethical behaviour of staff in vulnerable positions include fair selection and recruitment procedures, objective promotion criteria, opportunities for job rotation and enrichment, clear description of tasks, transparent division of responsibilities, separation of competencies, screening of staff, and sharing responsibilities among staff members[230]. However, also with respect to these instruments, there is surprisingly little evidence on the effectiveness of the different measures. Yet, the Member States have not done enough to evaluate and to compare among themselves the effectiveness of, for example, job rotation as an anti-corruption instrument.

230 See Bossaert/Demmke, Main challenges in the field of ethics and integrity in the EU Member States, op. cit.

7. EFFECTS OF ETHICS RULES ON ETHICAL BEHAVIOUR – MORE RULES, MORE EFFECTIVENESS?

A study by Demmke et al.[231] on rules and standards in the field of conflicts of interests for Holders of Public Services in the EU Member States revealed that many of the new Member States who joined the EU in 2004 and 2007 have more rules in place than the former EU-15 Member States. At the same time, a correlation between corruption levels and the level of integrity did not show that higher regulated countries have lower levels of corruption. These results indicate that other factors play a role as regards the degree of corruption. For example, the need to regulate ethics also depends on the level of trust in the public service. The more trust exists, the less regulation is needed. This may be one of the explanatory factors why high trust countries like the Scandinavian States have a relatively low level of regulation concerning conflicts of interests.

In this study we asked the Member States whether more rules, standards, controls, support, etc. are still needed as regards specific policies. The results showed that generally the Member States do not see a need for more rules with the exception of anti-corruption rules (see Table 18). The New Member States indicated somewhat higher need for more rules than the former EU-15 Member States. This need was mostly expressed as regards new rules in the fight against corruption and in public procurement. The former EU-15 countries express the strongest need for more rules in the field of post-employment.

Table 18. Are more rules and standards still needed?
(1=needed, 5= not needed)

	Old Member State	New Member State	Total
corruption	3,57	2,50	3,08
post-employment	3,36	3,00	3,19
politicisation	3,50	2,92	3,23
public procurement	4,00	3,00	3,54
abusing organisational resources	4,07	3,00	3,58
mobbing	4,00	3,17	3,60
fraud	3,93	3,25	3,62
gift policies	4,07	3,58	3,85
sexual intimidation	4,14	3,50	3,85

231 Demmke/ Bovens/Henökl/Moilanen, Regulating conflicts of interest for holders of public office in the European Union, op. cit.

Thus, despite a relatively high level of regulation, our results show that some Member States still see a need for more rules in some areas. However, especially the older EU-15 Member States are also of the opinion that, generally, new rules and standards are not needed. This may also be an indicator for the emergence of a new trend in which the Member States start to shift from a focus on rule adoption to the implementation and enforcement of the existing rules and standards.

7.1 Positive aspects of rules and standards in the field of ethics

Most supporters of better governance and more transparency, accountability, openness, and better rules and ethical standards also claim that transparency and rules and standards are important because government employees and Holders of Public Office hold positions of such importance that the public can claim a reasonable right to regulate more, and also because the public want to know some of the details of their professional activities and personal finances and the potential conflicts those might create. Especially in the field of post-employment, registers of financial interest, requirements for more transparency and declaration of information, etc. reveal important information to the public which would otherwise be kept in secret. Mostly, partisans in favour of more or better rules do not pretend that more rules and standards will decrease corruption and conflicts of interest. However, additional standards may deter public officials and Holders of Public Office from questionable behaviour! More or better-designed rules are also meant to eliminate the sometimes arbitrary practices and privileges inherited from the past. Particularly highly regulated countries and institutions face the challenge of a poor quality of rules, overlapping rules and a low level of awareness of the existing rules and standards (which are mostly not codified into one document but fragmented over several documents). However, awareness is growing about the need to codify and integrate different legal approaches into new ethics infrastructures.

Most Member States indicate the need for more rules, standards and controls in a number of policies and as regards a number of instruments. However, some countries mention the need for a better enforcement of the existing rules. For example, the Netherlands state "that there is no need for more rules. In line with the recommendations made by Greco, some amendments will be made to our laws relating to the financing of political parties". Also, the European Commission stresses that "there is no need for more rules, but reinforcement in advice and support could be welcome, depending also on available resources". Next, Austria mentions that there is no need for more but clearer rules. Similarly, Sweden argues that it is not so much rules, rather than the practice that counts. Overall, the new Member States express a greater need for more rules and standards than the old Member States. This is in contradiction with a study by Demmke et al.[232] for the European Commission, which came to the conclusion that – as regards the regulation of Holders of Public Office - the new Member States have already more rules in place than the old Member States.

Despite these limitations, most Member States are asking for more rules and policies, especially in the field of corruption (see Table 18 on page 127). This is in line with our findings on the focus of public discussions which is mostly on corruption issues. Thus, many Member States are under pressure to adopt more rules in the field of corruption because the public and the media require these measures.

Interestingly, the call for more rules and policies in the field of post-employment rules contradicts somewhat with the expected effects of post-employment rules, which are seen rather sceptically. Hence, post-employment issues are becoming more important. On the other hand, the Member States are uncertain how to effectively manage post-employment issues. We were also surprised to see that many Member States are of the opinion that more rules, standards and controls are needed in the field of politicization. Is this an indicator that politicization is back on the agenda and becomes, once again, an issue of growing importance?
Overall, the supporters of more and better rules and ethical standards claim that rules and standards are important because Holders of Public Office and public officials "hold positions of such importance and such accountability that the public can claim a reasonable right to know some of the details of their personal finances and the potential conflicts those might create"[233].

Especially in the field of registers of financial interest, requirements for more transparency and declaration of information, etc. reveal important information to the public which would otherwise be kept secret. For example, in the United States a study from the Center for Public Integrity shows that "more than 28 percent of state legislators who reported their finances sat on a committee with authority over at least one of their personal interests in 2001 (...). Eighteen percent disclosed ties to organisations registered to lobby state governments. And 10 percent were employed by other government agencies..."[234]. The publication

---

232 Demmke/ Bovens/Henökl/Moilanen, Regulating conflicts of interest for holders of public office in the European Union, op. cit.

233 G. S. Mackenzie, Scandal proof: Do ethics laws make government better? Brookings Institution, Washington D.C , 2002, p. 168.

234 David Dagan, Personal politics: All too often legislators' private interests are hidden from private view. Special report, 24 September 2004. Center of Public Integrity, 2004.

of these figures may not be sufficient to discipline office holders and improve ethical behaviour because public exposure acts as a stimulus. However, only the fact that public disclosure is not hidden from public view enables the public to control the public services and politicians at all.

The same argument can be used for strict regulations on gift policies. Apart from the regulation of general ethical principles, gifts and related benefits are by far the most regulated item in the field of conflicts of interest. Our study shows that only 14% of all institutions have no regulations in the field of gifts. Almost all Courts of Auditors and Central Banks that contributed to our study have rules in this field. In the literature some authors suggest that laws of ethics that had "the greatest impact on the legislative process are those that ban or limit gifts (…) from lobbyists or their principals, or laws that simply require their disclosure. In most states these laws have reduced gift giving and gift taking"[235]. "Gift bans and gift disclosure requirements have been highly effective."[236]

Other positive effects of rules and standards are that they contribute to transforming cultures. One example is the British example of the Seven Principles of Public Life[237], which is one of the few European standards of ethics applicable to all Holders of Public Service. The Seven Principles were set out by the Committee on Standards in Public Life and became a well-known standards document – also on the international level. The seven principles are:

- **Selflessness**. Holders of public office should act solely in terms of the public interest. They should not do so in order to gain financial or other benefits for themselves, their family or their friends.
- **Integrity**. Holders of public office should not place themselves under any financial or other obligation to outside individuals or organisations that might seek to influence them in the performance of their official duties.
- **Objectivity**. In carrying out public business, including making public appointments, awarding contracts, or recommending individuals for rewards and benefits, holders of public office should make choices on merit.
- **Accountability**. Holders of public office are accountable for their decisions and actions to the public and must submit themselves to whatever scrutiny is appropriate to their office.

235 Saint-Martin/Thompson, Public ethics and governance, op. cit., p. 172.
236 Ibid.
237 http://www.public-standards.gov.uk, last time checked on 26.3.2012.

- **Openness**. Holders of public office should be as open as possible about all the decisions and actions that they take. They should give reasons for their decisions and restrict information only when the wider public interest clearly demands it.
- **Honesty**. Holders of public office have a duty to declare any private interests relating to their public duties and to take steps to resolve any conflicts arising in a way that protects the public interest.
- **Leadership.** Holders of public office should promote and support these principles by leadership and example.

Mostly, partisans in favour of more or better rules do not pretend that more rules and standards will decrease corruption and conflicts of interest. However, additional standards may deter HPOs from questionable behaviour. More or better-designed rules are also meant to eliminate the sometimes arbitrary practices and privileges inherited from the past. The process of accessions of the new Member States to the EU in 2004 and 2007 had the positive effect that all new Member States reformed their laws on ethics, corruption and conflicts of interest. Today, the regulation density is higher in these countries than in the former member countries. This is certainly a positive development. In the meantime, most of the new Member States have introduced more and stricter rules for all governmental institutions. Despite all the problems in implementing and enforcing these rules, this can be considered as a positive process.

In addition, the process of elaborating rules and codes of standards may have important educational effects. "It would be unfortunate if the emphasis on a code of ethics as a product obscured the value of the process by which a code is developed and subsequently revised. This process is a time of critical self-examination by both individual members and the profession as a whole. The profession must institutionalise a process whereby its moral commitments are regularly discussed and assessed in the light of changing conditions, both inside and outside the profession. The widespread participation of members in such an effort helps to reinvigorate and bring into sharp focus the underlying values and moral commitments of their profession. It is a time of testing one's professional ethics against those of colleagues and for testing the profession's ethics against the experience of its members and the values of society. This process of self-criticism, codification, and consciousness-raising reinforces or redefines the profession's collective responsibility and is an important learning and maturing experience for both individual members and the profession."[238]

238 Mark S. Frankel, Professional codes, why, how and with what impact?, in: Journal of Business Ethics. Volume 8, Numbers 2-3/1989, pp. 112-113.

So far, only few studies have demonstrated a clear connection between rules and standards in the field of conflicts of interests and a decrease in conflicts. However, a study by Fain shows that strict zero gift policies have a positive impact on gift taking. Strict gift policies may seem extreme by prohibiting public officials from receiving gifts from anyone. However, they eliminate any doubt, are easy to understand and also easy to enforce[239].

Other experts claim that "strict rules, standards and management instruments in the field of conflicts of interest bring other benefits for public sector organisations. First and foremost, opportunities for corruption or improper conduct are reduced. Second, effective policies and procedures for identifying, disclosing and managing conflicts of interest mean that unfounded accusations of bias can be dealt with more easily and efficiently. Third, the organisation can demonstrate its commitment to good governance by addressing an issue that is commonly associated with corruption and misconduct. Fourth, a transparent system that is observed by everyone in an organisation as a matter of course will also demonstrate to members of the public and others who deal with the organisation that its proper role is performed in a way that is fair and unaffected by improper considerations. Failure to identify, declare and manage a conflict of interest is where serious corruption often begins and this is why managing conflicts of interest is such an important corruption prevention strategy."[240]

Another empirical study by Feldheim and Wang demonstrates that ethical behaviour of public officials improves public trust. The authors find higher levels of public trust in cities where managers have higher perceptions of ethical behaviour. Furthermore, "integrity, openness, and loyalty to the public interest (...) are crucial in increasing public trust"[241]. The importance of good governance and ethical administration belongs to the daily public management rhetoric which is stressed by politicians and civil servants. Today, ethical requirements imposed onto governments, administrations and public officials are continuously increasing. Thus, it seems that never before have governments and public authorities invested as much in the fight against corruption, the establishment of ethical infrastructures, ethics training and in the adoption of new rules in order to curb corruption levels, fight against discrimination and – more generally – in order to improve ethical cultures and ethical behaviour. Consequently, there are

---

239 Herbert Fain, The case for a zero gift policy, in: Public Integrity, Vol. 4, No. 1/2002, p. 61.

240 Independent Commission against Corruption and Crime, Managing public ethics in the public sector, Guidelines, Australia, Sydney 2004.

241 M.A Feldheim/X.Wang, Ethics and public trust, in: Public Integrity, 2003-2004, Vol. 6, No. 1/2004, p. 73.

more rules, procedures and monitoring procedures in place than ever before. Whereas in the past only a restricted number of issues were seen as unethical (and consequently they were sanctioned), today the definition of unethical behaviour concerns an ever growing number of issues, such as:

- Bribing (misuse of public power for private gain);
- Favouritism (nepotism, cronyism, patronage);
- Fraud and theft of resources;
- Conflict of interest through gifts (asking, offering, accepting);
- Conflict of interest through sideline activities (secondary jobs, other financial interests);
- No/partial registration of information on conflicts of interest;
- Violation of post-employment rules;
- Violation of oath;
- Improper use of authority (gifts, allowances, gratifications);
- Misuse and manipulation of information (cheating or concealing information, breaching confidentiality of information);
- Indecent treatment of colleagues, citizens or customers (discrimination based on gender, race, or sexual orientation; intimidation and sexual harassment; bullying, nagging, gossiping);
- Waste and abuse of organisational resources (e.g., private use of the Internet);
- Misconduct in private time (e.g., driving under influence of alcohol or drugs);
- Wrong permitting;
- Sickness leaves while healthy;
- Not following orders or procedures;
- Violation of fair and merit based procedures;
- Private travelling at the expense of the organisation.

Our study shows also that more than half of the Member States continue to define more issues as subjects for unethical behaviour (see Table 19 on page 134). On the other hand, there is actually no country that deregulates ethics policies. In addition, almost all Member States revise their ethics policies on a regular basis.

Table 19. Are more issues defined as subjects for unethical behaviour?

(Frequencies in parenthesis)

	Relative frequency
Very much	0 (0)
Somewhat	56 (14)
No changes	35 (9)
Cannot say	12 (3)
Decreased	0 (0)
Total	100 (26)

On the other hand, experts comment on the effectiveness of instruments in the field very differently and represent an even broader spectrum of views. In the field of conflicts of interest, some argue that a public reporting system is unnecessary and that requiring the filing and review of confidential reports would sufficiently prevent financial conflicts of interests. Others believe that public scrutiny is essential to deterring potential conflicts of interest and to encouraging confidence in government. As Stark states, "We now prophylactically prohibit all officials from entering into an ever-increasing number of specified, factually ascertainable sets of circumstances because they might lead to inner conflict"[242].

Ethics experts face many difficulties in answering whether ethical challenges are increasing, decreasing – or both? According to a recent study by de Schrijver et al. concerning Belgium's Flemish public sector, the most common types of unethical behaviour include minimal effort by employees; gossiping; use of the Internet, e-mail, or telephone above the permitted standards; accepting small gifts from external parties, and falsely reporting sick. "Deliberately giving false information in reports and/or policy documents (…), accepting bribes (money or favours) to do or neglect something while at work (…), accepting gifts of more serious value from external parties (…), sexual intimidation (…) and selling confidential information to third parties, on the other hand, are less often observed"[243]. Moreover, different forms of unethical behaviour have a different acceptance in different administrative cultures.

Another development is also striking: whereas the media and the wider public call for the introduction of more rules and standards in the field, many experts

---

242 Andrew Stark, Conflict of interest in American public life, Harvard, Cambridge, 2000, p. 264.

243 Annelis Schrijver/Karlien Delbeke/Jeroen Maesschalck/Stefaan Pleysier, Fairness perceptions and organisational misbehavor, op. cit, pp. 691-703.

discuss the potential negative effects of more standards, processes and rules, pointing, for example, to the fact that public discussions on ethics pay too little attention to the impact of ethics policies on administrative procedures, processes, monitoring requirements, costs and civil rights. The first experts to address these problematic issues in detail were Anechiarico and J.B. Jacobs[244] in the year 1996. Thus, literature on the challenges and paradoxes of conflict of interest policies is still fairly recent.

7.2 Critical aspects

Critics such as Anechiarico and Jacobs[245], Mackenzie[246], Stark[247], Saint-Martin and F.Thompson[248], Behncke[249] and Bovens[250], argue that more rules of ethics do not necessarily provide an efficient response to the decline of public trust and integrity issues, but may cause even more cynicism regarding public and political institutions. The problem, critics say, is that the expansion of ethics regulations and more public discussions about the need for more and better (conflict of interest) rules have not contributed to a rise in public confidence in government. In fact, the calls for more and better ethics may have the opposite effect. More "ethics regulations and more ethics enforcers have produced more ethics investigations and prosecutions... Whatever the new ethics regulations may have accomplished... they have done little to reduce publicity and public controversy about the ethical behaviour of public officials"[251].

Most ethics experts are indeed of the opinion that more rules, even if well managed, may not automatically build more trust. Contrary to this, new rules may decrease public trust "by generating a sense that all lawmakers are fundamentally untrustworthy"[252]. The most prominent case is the situation in the United States, where "legions of lawyers and journalists earn their living from ethics lawsuits and scandals. In particular after scandals, a new wave of conflict of in-

---

244 Antechiarico/Jacobs, The Pursuit of Absolute Integrity, op. cit., p. 12.
245 Ibid.
246 G.S. Mackenzie, Scandal proof, op. cit.
247 Stark, Conflict of Interest in American Public Life, op. cit.
248 Saint-Martin/Thompson, Public Ethics and Governance, op. cit.
249 Nathalie Behnke, Monitoring public administrators or signalling trustworthiness to the demos? The two functions of ethics regulations, in: Polis 61, University of Hagen, 2006.
250 Mark Bovens, Het ongelijk van Dales. Bestuurskunde, Vol. 15, No. 1/2006, pp. 64-74.
251 Mackenzie, Scandal proof, op. cit. p. 112.
252 B.A. Rosenson, The costs and benefits of ethics laws, in: Saint-Martin & Thompson, Public Ethics and Governance, op. cit., p. 137.

terest, financial disclosure or gift acceptance regulations seemed to be the appropriate way to re-establish public trust by signalling that "something was being done." These ethics measures have mostly been introduced by politicians with an eye on the perceived problem of decreasing public trust. The intention of increasing public trust, however, was never met in reality. Quite to the contrary, meanwhile the ethics infrastructure in the US has reached a level in which it contributes to further undermining public trust....The complaint about scandals, corruption and low ethical standards always seems justified and the promise to establish higher standards is always likely to be a promising means to gain votes. Similarly, most presidential candidates from Dwight D. Eisenhower to Bill Clinton tried to gain profile by emphasising the "ethics gap" and announcing uniform and higher standards of behaviour for the federal government, tightening post-employment restrictions or enlarging the financial disclosure requirements."[253]

As Behnke shows, "in spite of the individual rationality of these strategies, the collective irrationality lies in the fact that ever more transparency, ever higher standards and tighter regulations create ever more violations of ethical rules, more scandals and more investigations, thus undermining the legitimacy of the institution and destroying public trust and creating collective costs that far outweigh the individual benefits. In addition to the individual rationality leading to collective irrationality, the last element that makes the situation a real Prisoners' Dilemma is the fact that no built-in mechanism can stop this arms race."[254] The assumption on the part of the legislators and Members of Government who favour the adoption of new rules and standards is that this will have a positive effect and increase public trust in Government. However, a strong focus on ethics, too strict approaches, too much publicity and too many rules may also undermine public trust in the short-run.

7.3 Costs of ethics and fight against corruption

During the last decades, costs for ethics policies have been rising in the USA and in Canada. Almost every state has special ethics committees and monitoring bodies at its disposal. A study estimated that in the USA there are nearly 15,000 full- and part-time ethics officials in the federal executive branch[255]. Still, there

---

253 Nathalie Behnke, Ethics as apple pie: The arms race of ethical standards in congressional and presidential campaigns. EGPA-Paper presented at the conference on Ethics and Integrity of Governance: A transatlantic dialogue in Leuven in June 2005, pp. 1-2.

254 Ibid., p. 3.

255 Menzel, Ethics Management, op. cit.

is very little evidence about the overall costs for ethics policies and financial, organisational and personnel costs of regulations, standard setting, management, monitoring and training. In our study we tried to shed some light on this issue, as we expected that some trends in the field of ethics mirror the developments on the other side of the Atlantic. In fact, costs may still be by far lower than in the USA and in Canada. However, the costs are increasing the more the Member States agree to establish ethics infrastructure systems and invest in monitoring bodies, training, the implementation of new rules and procedures.

Our hypotheses were twofold. First, we estimated that costs are rising. Second, we assumed that there is very little information about the actual costs because of the high degree of fragmentation and decentralisation of those actors and bodies that are in charge of ethics (and consequently, bear the costs). Costs estimations should integrate different costs for training, disclosure policies, the management of ethics committees, risks assessments and integrity violations. They should also cover cost-benefit evaluations: what are the benefits of ethical employees, ethical organisations and ethics infrastructure? How much money can be saved if employees perceive their organisations as fair, enjoy ethical leadership and act accordingly?

As regards the answers of the Member States, we could not confirm our first hypothesis. However, our second hypothesis was partly confirmed. In fact, no Member States had estimations about the cost developments in the field. There were no evaluations about costs and benefits of ethics policies carried out. We found only some cost evaluations from the United Kingdom and from Ireland. As regards the UK, the budget for the British Committee on Standards in Public Life was estimated at 636,000 pounds for the year 2010/2011. In Ireland, "the cost of operating the Standards in Public Office Commission in 2010 was EUR 862,000. Additionally, there is the cost of implementing the ethics framework in parliament, ministries and public bodies. As this is accounted for as part of general administrative overhead in personnel units, specific ethics-related costs would not be available".

Some Member States stated that the costs for ethics policies are limited. For example, the Netherlands mentioned that their ethics system is not cost-intensive. Most costly will be the organisation of ethics training and risk assessments. Also disciplinary investigations can be cost-intensive if compared to the cost of the specific integrity violations, but not if compared with the necessity of upholding public values and trust in government. Thus, according to the Dutch position, one could say that the costs for the regulation and management of ethics are justified if, as a result, important and costly scandals will be avoided. Also France considered that there were no significant specific costs beyond the normal operation of training and of the legal system costs. Greece replied: “Ethics policies are low cost”.

Slightly different is the situation in the European Commission: ”We do not have such estimations for the time being. Nevertheless, ethics policies, even if they are not cost-intensive, require a certain level of resources. In addition, if transparency is considered as one of the elements, the cost is higher as the implementation of Regulation 1049/2001 entails a substantial workload for the services". Despite the limited evidence on cost developments, we propose for the future to have an eye on the development of costs in the area of ethics and to establish cost-benefit evaluations.

8. OUTCOMES: THE RISE OF PUBLIC SERVICE ETHICS AND GOOD GOVERNANCE

In the last decades governments have become ever more active in introducing new accountability mechanisms, ethical standards, antidiscrimination rules, diversity policies, transparency policies, citizen orientation programs, etc. Because the principles of good governance are such prized political and administrative values, the usual assumption has been that there can never be too much of it[256]. Consequently, the meaning of ethics has consistently widened over the years[257]. For example, in the field of managing conflicts of interests, more governments have moved from managing conflicts of interests through top-down approaches (prohibitions, restrictions, criminal and administrative sanctions) to more complex approaches including education, training, transparency requirements, introducing preventive policies (regulating post-employment) and better monitoring systems.

Despite the existence of, in many cases very impressive, ethics management systems and numerous laws, regulations and codes in place, the Member States of the EU continue to define more issues as unethical. Despite this trend, there is little evidence about the effectiveness of ethics rules. If the public service is to function effectively in an increasingly fluid and globalised environment, where working conditions and external circumstances change rapidly, it must be able to work with a wide range of sectors including private enterprise, the non-profit or third sector, and the citizenry.

This has three crucial, interrelated implications for public sector ethics. Firstly, public sector employees must be able to make the right ethical decisions in all situations. This will become even more of a challenge when they have to work in partnership with people and organisations with different cultures, different ways of working and, in some cases, different ethical outlooks and priorities. Secondly, public employees need to deal with the reality that the Public Service is no longer a closed organisation. Thirdly, public employers must recognize that, as a result of employment policies, labour market pressures and other changes over the last decade, people with a variety of previous experiences in different employment cultures are moving into the public services. As a consequence, the public services can no longer rely solely on long term workplace socialisation to ensure that staff understand and apply public service ethical

256 Paul G. Thomas, Introduction, in: Guy Peters/Jon Pierre, Handbook of public administration, Sage, 2003, p. 549.

257 Ibid., p. 550.

standards. Therefore, we believe that induction training and especially regulation and management of post-employment issues will become more important.

Also ethics policies are still becoming more important everywhere. The underlying reasons for this worldwide development can be summarized as follows. Firstly, Governments are expected to ensure that public officials do not allow their private interests to compromise official decision-making. Secondly, society is becoming increasingly demanding as to the behaviour of Holders of Public Office and public officials. Consequently, potential conflicts of interest may weaken public trust. Thirdly, political scandals and more media attention put additional pressure on the different actors to do even more in the field of ethics.

People expect Holders of Public Office and public officials to have very high standards of integrity because they have more power, influence and decision-making discretion than any private persons (apart from managers in multinational companies and banks). They exercise public powers on behalf of the country. They spend public money for important governmental projects. They raise taxes. They take decisions which have an impact on the fundamental rights of the citizens. They decide on health and on risk protection. For all these important tasks, it is important that they exercise their role properly, and act lawfully, honestly and loyally without acquiring any personal advantage. Because of this, standards of integrity must be set at high levels. A study conducted by Gaugler in Germany shows that the higher the prestige and the position of a Holder of Public Office, the more companies and organisations seek to establish contact, offer memberships in boards, etc. Accordingly, former cabinet members frequently assume important positions or functions in companies and organisations after they have left office[258]. In recognising this, it seems appropriate that specific rules and standards should regulate the behaviour of Holders of Public Office but not necessarily ordinary civil servants. When designing ethical instruments these differences must be taken into account[259]. The call to regulate post-employment issues more strongly for former Members of Government also stems from these differences.

Things become more complex when comparing the different categories of Holders of Public Office and public officials: they have different positions and tasks, enjoy different degrees of media attention, have different powers and work in different organisational, institutional, political and legal settings. Thus, standards

258 M. Gaugler, Bundestagsabgeordnete zwischen Mandat und Aufsichtsrat, VDM, Saarbrücken, 2006, p. 108.
259 Behncke, Ethics as apple pie, op. cit., p. 8.

of integrity should be somewhat different according to the different positions. This also implies that different ethics instruments should be applicable to the different positions. But is this still of interest for citizens and the media?

8.1 Ethics as moral policy

Today, not a day goes by without extensive media coverage of corruption, fraud and unethical behaviour of Holders of Public Office and public employees. It seems that public reporting about ethical scandals and ethical difficulties are even increasing. How is this related to public trust? Will public trust decrease as a consequence of reports on scandals? Did, as a consequence of the introduction of new laws, regulations and codes, the ethical behaviour of public officials and Holders of Public Office improve? Did corruption and conflicts of interest decrease? Is more care taken for ethical leadership and ethical cultures? Is deviant behaviour of employees and misbehaviour in organisations being reduced? What is the added value of ethics laws and policies in changing organisational cultures? And what about public expectations towards political leadership and growing criticism against authorities? Are expectations rising, and will thus lead to a slow but steady decline of political authority?

The more rules and standards are introduced, the more often rules and standards can be violated. Consequently, media and the public may interpret this as a sign of declining ethical standards. "Thus, rather than decreasing the number of cases of unethical behaviour, by declaring behaviour unethical which was formerly in accordance with the rules, the absolute number of scandals and cases of unethical behaviour increases, thus creating the appearance of public officials becoming more unethical"[260].

In fact, during the last decades, the public standard of morality has become much stricter. Previously tolerated conduct is now deemed unethical and previously unethical conduct is now deemed criminal. Whereas in the past, only a restricted number of issues were seen as unethical (and consequently they were sanctioned), today the definition of unethical behaviour concerns an ever growing number of issues. Consequently, the policies on ethics and the discussions about needs for reforms have become more open and more complex, but also more driven by scandals and media interest. As Table 2 on page 57 shows, majority of the countries say that public discussions on ethics are scandal-driven (42%). Others are somewhere in between (39%), and only the Netherlands has reported that their debates are more value-driven (15%).

---

260 Ibid.

From a political point of view, it may be difficult to be against new initiatives and new rules. Regulating ethics policies is popular. Consequently, being against more rules and standards is risky. Also our study shows that no country has deregulated ethics policies. Contrary to this: most Member States are still in the process of re-regulating ethics. On the other hand, ethics policies are becoming more and more politicised. Ethics is slowly emerging as a perfect policy field in electoral campaigns. Politicians can be sure that calls for new initiatives will be applauded by the citizenry because these calls reflect a widespread perception in European societies that levels of corruption and conflicts of interest are increasing and something must be done. From the point of view of a Holder of Public Office, it would not only be detrimental to be against new or even higher ethical standards. In fact, the call for higher ethical standards and tighter rules of ethics are more and more the subject of election campaigns in many countries.

The downside of this development is that it becomes more difficult to avoid that ethics, as a policy issue, is abused as moral stigmatisation. More and more politicians use accusations of unethical conduct as a political and moral instrument. Rules of ethics in particular are resources that politicians mobilise to attack and discredit their opponents. Consequently, ethics is increasingly used as a political and moral instrument with the aim of denouncing political opponents. Ethics is also increasingly linked with moral arguments. Despite the fact that rules which regulate conflicts of interest should not involve moral judgments on ethics, laws are also becoming a "moral measurement" and people and the media "place stigma" on public officials and Holders of Public Office who violate them.

8.2 Ethics and trust developments

Today, it is increasingly popular to link the discussions on ethics with those about the development of public trust. Many people believe that more rules and standards bring higher levels of public trust. In reality, the concept of public trust is very complex[261]. For example, whereas many observers believe that levels of public trust are constantly decreasing, the reality is that levels of public trust vary from country to country and from institution to institution. Levels of public trust also fluctuate.

The results of our study show different features. First, most Member States are of the opinion that trust levels decrease. Second, trust levels decrease more as

---

261 Steven van de Walle, Perceptions of administrative performance: The key to trust in government? Dissertation, University of Leuven, No. 79, 2004.

regards the political class than as regards public officials. Third, trust levels are related to the economic performance of a country: the higher the general government deficit, the lower the trust levels (see Table 20).

Table 20. Effect of financial crisis on trust levels

(1=increased trust, 5=decreased trust)

General government deficit/surplus 2010 (percentage of GDP)	Politicians	Civil servants
High deficit (> -7.0%)	4.38	3.50
Middle-level deficit (-7.0% to -4.2%)	3.44	3.22
Low-level deficit (< -4.2%)	3.00	2.89
Total	3.68	3.20

Still, these results do not show how ethics is related to trust. For example, Bovens and Wille[262] discuss ten different factors that have an impact on the level of public trust: performance of the public sector, general perceptions of the government, the economic situation, scandals and dramas, media reporting, change of political culture, changing expectations, emergence of a new generation with different values, changing role of middle class. Bovens and Wille come to the conclusion that the perception of the policies of the government has the strongest impact on sudden changes of public trust.

According to Robbins[263], trust is a positive expectation that the other party does not act opportunistically through words, actions, or decisions. When we trust someone, we are willing to take the risk and put ourselves in a vulnerable position. Trust builds over time, and it is based on relevant but limited samples of experience. Trust has five main components: integrity (honesty and truthfulness), competence (technical and interpersonal knowledge and skills), consistency (reliability, predictability, and good judgment in handling situations), loyalty (willingness to protect and save face for another person) and openness (reliance on receiving the full truth). However, if integrity is missing, the remaining four factors are meaningless. Perceived trust affects the ways how leader receives information and how staff cooperates with her/him. Sharing of information presumes that the second party does not misuse the information against the rights and interests of the first party. If there is a lack of trust between employ-

262 Mark Bovens/A. Wille, Waar bleef het vertrouwen in de overheid? Bestuurskunde, Vol. 15, 4/2006, p. 50.

263 Stephen Robbins, Essentials of organisational behaviour. Pearson/Prentice Hall, 2005.

ees and management, parties do not inform each other and the flow of information is blocked.

Robbins distinguishes three types of trust: (1) deterrence-based trust, which is based on fear of reprisal if the trust is violated; (2) knowledge-based trust, where trust is based on behavioural predictability which stems from a history of interaction; and (3) identification-based trust, which is based on a mutual understanding of each other's intentions and appreciation of the other's wants and desires. Robbins argues that the key issues for building trust are the following: practice openness (share information), be fair (praise when relevant, assess objectively, pay attention to equality), speak about emotions (be human), tell the truth (do not lie or hide relevant information), be consistent, fulfil promises, maintain confidentiality, practice competence[264].

Trust and integrity are the cornerstones of a democratic, open society. Basically, trust is a trait of deserving confidence. Trustworthiness is a moral value. Citizens' trust in public institutions is a complex issue. Here, one may refer to "Jeremy Bentham's classic statement, according to which every good political institution is a system of distrust, because politicians have authority and the temptation to abuse it. That is why we can ask: are politicians and public sector leaders trustworthy? One single factor explaining the trust does not exist. Those who are involved in politics might think more of their own welfare than the welfare of citizens. Secondly, a high level of trust in one institution tends to extend to other institutions. Thirdly, in general terms, corruption decreases trust in institutions"[265]. As far as it concerns our focus, we share the opinion that the relationship between trust and integrity violations is rather complicated than simple[266]. Do perceptions of trust determine the views of integrity violations or vice versa?

Trust can be studied through different dimensions: trust between individuals, trust towards the activity of professionals, trust inside and within organisations, trust between organisations, trust in politicians, or trust inside the community[267]. When talking about trust, it is good to remember that it is a question of citizens' emotions, beliefs, opinions and experiences shaped through many processes.

---

264 Ibid.

265 M. E. Warren, Democracy and deceit: Regulating appearances of corruption, in: American Journal of Political Science, Vol. 50, No. 1/2006, pp. 162-174.

266 Steven van de Walle/S. van Roosbroek/Geert Bouckaert, Trust in the public sector: Is there any evidence for a long-term decline?, in: International Review of Administrative Sciences, Vol. 74, No. 1/2008, pp. 215-216.

267 Alan Lawton/Alan Doig, Researching ethics for public service organizations: The view from Europe, in: Public Integrity, Vol. 8, 1/2006, pp. 16-17.

Some of the opinions are already formulated as youngsters through the process of socialization.

Trust in the organisation is built on the employee's belief that since current organisational decisions are fair, future organisational decisions will be fair. The continuance of employee trust in the organisation and the organisation continuing to meet the employee's expectations of fairness creates the reciprocal relationship between trust and organisational justice[268]. Research has found that procedural justice is the strongest predictor of organisational trust[269]. A positive relationship between an employee and supervisor can lead to trust in the organisation[270].

All distrust is not harmful. A certain amount of distrust is healthy and functional: it is needed to maintain the level of administrative accountability. The optimal level of trust depends on the development of political and administrative culture. A certain level of trust may be high in one but low in another country[271]. There is no single or unambiguous explanation why some organisations seem to be trustworthy, while others do not. It is a question of personal experience, of the experience of the circle of acquaintances, of images and of the history and base of the trustor[272].

In spite of the positive intention of good governance concepts, ever more transparency, ever higher standards and tighter regulations may also create ever more violations of ethical rules, more scandals and more investigations, thus undermining the legitimacy of the institution and weakening public trust and creating collective costs that far outweigh the individual benefits. The assumption on the

---

268 James B. DeConinck, The effect of organizational justice, perceived organizational support, and perceived supervisor support on marketing employees' level of trust, in: Journal of Business Research, Vol. 63, No. 12/2010, pp. 1349–1355.

269 Yochi Cohen-Charasha/Paul E. Spector, The role of justice in organizations: A meta-analysis, in: Organizational Behavior and Human Decision Processes, Vol. 86, No. 2/2001, pp. 278–321; Anne P. Hubbell/Rebecca M. Chory-Assad, Motivating factors: Perceptions of justice and their relationship with managerial and organizational trust, in: Communication Studies, Vol. 56, No. 1/2005, pp. 47-70.

270 Joy H. Karriker/Margaret L. Williams, Organizational justice and organizational citizenship behavior: A mediated multifoci model, in: Journal of Management, Vol. 35, No. 1/2009, pp. 112-135.

271 Van de Walle et al. (2008), op. cit., 52; see also Geert Hofstede, Culture's consequences – comparing values, behaviors, institutions and organizations across nations, second edition, Thousand Oaks, London, New Delhi, 2001.

272 Van de Walle et al. (2008), op. cit., pp. 224–225; Salminen, Ethical governance, op. cit., p. 43.

part of the public employees, legislators and Members of Government who favour the adoption of new rules and standards is that this will have a positive effect and increase public trust. However, a strong focus on new accountability mechanisms, transparency, participation, ethics, overly strict approaches, too much publicity and too many rules may also undermine public trust. Therefore, critics argue that more rules of ethics do not necessarily provide an efficient response to the decline of public trust and integrity issues but may cause even more cynicism regarding public and political institutions. The problem, critics say, is that the expansion of ethics regulations and more public discussions about the need for more and better (conflicts of interest) rules have not contributed to a rise in public confidence in government. In fact, the calls for more and better ethics can backfire.

8.3 Development of ethical behaviour

There have been three distinct trends in the ethics literature in the last decade. The first is a surge in ethics literature which focuses on scandals and the failures of politicians and public officials and, consequently, decreasing trust levels. The second trend is a sort of reaction to the many reforms, policies and instruments which were introduced as a response to the scandals. Here the focus is mostly on whether we now have 'too much' or 'too little' ethics rules. Ultimately, the argument goes that while costs associated with increased monitoring, oversight and control have risen, they have not, to this point at least, translated into higher trust levels and less ethics violations. The third trend is the broadening and diversification of the whole discussion. For example, whereas more experts discuss ethics in the context of good governance policies, others are interested in the institutionalization of ethics, the effects of different ethics instruments ethics and social justice perceptions as a result of administrative reforms.

Generally, the literature on scandals and political failures supports the thesis that unethical behaviour is increasing and trust levels are decreasing. On the other hand, claims that unethical behaviour is increasing and levels of public trust are decreasing are difficult to prove with hard facts. First, one should define what unethical behaviour is (which is not an easy task). Second, one should have clear standards about ethical behaviour (which is even more difficult to define). Third, the definition of (un-) ethical behaviour is subject of constant changes.

Mostly, critics of "too much ethics" believe that the rise in ethics policies and rules supports the perception that unethical behaviour is increasing since more rules and standards can be broken. However, an increasing number of violations are no indicator that different forms of unethical behaviour are increasing as such. Still, the higher the ethical requirements for public officials, legislators and ministers, the more likely it is that ethics will be abused for political reasons or – also – by the media. Only decades ago, fewer violations were detected because fewer rules were in place. However, it could well be that unethical behaviour was more frequent than today. For example, not long ago, politicians, Holders of Public Office and public officials were not suspected of having conflicts of interest when exercising additional honorary positions. Today, almost all outside activities are seen as sources of potential conflicts of interests.

The rise of ethical standards and expectations may also suggest that unethical behaviour is only increasing because of higher expectations. In reality, there are reasons to believe that ethical behaviour has improved. A study for the Slovenian EU Presidency showed that 41% of public employees believe that ethical violations are decreasing and ethical attitudes have improved. 31% think that the situation has not changed, and 29% consider that the situation has deteriorated[273]. However, this observation needs to be elaborated. Many respondents from the Eastern European countries were especially of the opinion that unethical behaviour is increasing, whereas respondents from Scandinavia and from Mediterranean countries said that unethical behaviour is decreasing. Other positive effects can also be noted. For example, the national administrations have become more transparent, less hierarchical, more accountable, more performance-oriented, more citizen-oriented, less discriminatory and more attentive to ethical problems.

Thus, it seems, judging the effects of ethics policies on ethical behaviour and the development of unethical behaviour is complicated. Despite the growing amount of literature, studies and policy recommendations, there is still no common understanding as regards the development of unethical behaviour. Demmke[274] suggests that dynamics, contradictions and unintentional side-effects of governmental reform processes produce less and more ethical challenges at the same time but in different HR areas and as regards different instruments. New reform initiative and changing concepts of governance always create new ethical challenges, new conflicts of interests and new forms of unethical behaviour. At the same time, new rules and standards, growing awareness and new policies also have a positive impact as to the effectiveness of measures. Overall, unethical

---

273 Demmke et al., Regulating conflicts of interest for Holders of Public Office in the European Union, op. cit.

274 Christoph Demmke, Ethik und Integrität in den öffentlichen Diensten in Europa. Journal for Public and Nonprofit Services, Vol. 29, No. 1/2006, p. 68.

behaviour seems to be decreasing in a number of fields such as sexual intimidation and discrimination[275].

Over the past few years especially ethical issues have been becoming also a political instrument. Ethics is also increasingly linked with moral arguments. Despite the fact that rules should not involve moral judgments on holders, ethics laws and standards are easily becoming a moral measurement and people and the media place stigma on those who violate them[276]. According to Stark, the "problem with conflict of interest law is that it has become a mortal stigmatisation when, in reality, it is just law."

Consequently, positive intentions can easily turn into unintentional and perverse effects. Therefore, a better balance is needed between effective rules and standards and the need to avoid too much scrutiny and suspicion. It is true that Holders of Public Office and public officials have an important public mission. At the same time they are watched, controlled, and monitored as never before. Thus, the danger is that ever more rules, tougher disclosure requirements, stricter monitoring structures, and additional transparency requirements will reveal more violations of rules and standards. Another related problem concerns the fact that if the new rules are poorly drafted or even trivial, then we create problems for no reason. However, this development produces the opposite of what rule-makers intend to achieve: public trust is decreasing because the citizens have the perception that their Holders of Public Office are less ethical than they were before. Ultimately, the price to be paid for the introduction of more rules and higher standards can also be even more of a public disappointment.

---

275 This observation is comparable to those made by Thompson in the United States, who observes that "ethics in Congress deserves greater attention not because members are more corrupt (they are not), not because citizens are more distrustful (they are), but because the institution itself continually poses new ethical challenges. The complexity of the institutional environment in which Members of Congress work invites more calls for accountability and creates new occasions for corruption. As the circumstances of potential corruption change, so too must the institutions of actual enforcement." See Thompson, Overcoming the Conflict of Interest in Congressional Ethics, op. cit.

276 Stark, Conflict of interest in American public life, op. cit., p. 266.

9. CONCLUSIONS

If in the past there were seen to be regulatory gaps and a lack of enforcement in the field of public-sector ethics, the more recent concern is that some governments may have gone overboard in building an elaborate ethics apparatus that reflects the prevailing negative assumptions about the motivations and capabilities of both politicians and public servants. Our findings confirm that these concerns are valid. On the one hand, ethics policies have become more complex. On the other hand, institutional and enforcement structures are still weak.

Today, trying to be ethical in every sense of the word could mean that public organisations and their leaders end up pleasing no one. The issue at the heart of this new ethics debate is whether there is too little, too much or just the right amount of ethics, with little consideration whether some policies and instruments effective, and whether more or less rules, sanctions and/or incentives are really needed.

Ethics policies often follow a fairly simple logic: the more public and media scrutiny, the more discovered political scandals and conflicts of interests, the more failure is attributed to too little control, not enough monitoring and not enough law[277]. Calling for new rules and standards is in most cases an easy response to a complex challenge. Consequently, there are more rules, procedures and monitoring procedures in place than ever before. This trend towards new ethics laws, rules, standards and monitoring systems runs counter to one of the most important reform trends, the reduction of administrative burdens and bureaucracy. So far no country has removed, reduced or abolished ethics standards as deregulating ethics policies would be highly unpopular.

During the current decade, in the media and on the political level, public-service ethics has received more attention than ever before. There has been enormous activity to create new ethics policies, instruments, structures and codes. Whereas in the past, only a restricted number of issues were seen as unethical and sanctioned, today the definition of unethical behaviour concerns an ever growing number of issues (see page 133).

Conduct which previously was tolerated becomes unacceptable. The concepts of corruption and conflict of interest have expanded to embrace more types of conduct. Also, the concepts of discrimination and mobbing have become broader than before. Finally, investigative technology, financial reporting, auditing and

---

277 Anechiarico/Jacobs, The pursuit of absolute integrity, op. cit., p. 12.

accountability mechanisms have become more intensive, complex and comprehensive.

The fight against unethical behaviour can only be understood against a cultural - social, legal, political and psychological - background. This background is somewhat ambivalent and controversial. Conceptions about unethical conduct are constantly developing. "In the last decade, the public standards of morality has become more strict"[278], and the gap between the political system and the implementing system much wider. This study cannot give objective answers as to whether we have too many or too few ethics rules, or, what the precise impact of the ethics rules is on trust, democracy, performance and behaviour. Today, work in the public sector is more individual, value-laden, emotional, pluralistic, unpredictable and therefore contentious than is allowed for in a dichotomous 'too much'/'too little'[279].

Ethics policies have indeed become more professional but also more complex and, in some cases, ineffective. However, deregulating ethics may render counterproductive results. There may be even good reasons to introduce new rules and policies, for example in the field of post-employment in some countries and/or institutions. As Demmke et al.[280] showed, the national parliaments are the least regulated systems. It is difficult to say whether unethical behaviour is increasing. Whereas some experts claim that unethical behaviour is increasing because of the effects of new management trends, the introduction of austerity measures, value changes, etc., others believe that the opposite is the case: especially from a historical point of view unethical behaviour and corruption have rather decreased.

In fact, the situation is even more complex. The rise of ethics is also a direct answer to new challenges, threats and complexities in the field. However, it is also a reaction to the increased power of the media, scandal-driven discourses and enhanced expectations of the citizenry. Moreover, the differentiation of ethics policies is also an answer to the individualization of new managerial and HR approaches.

---

278 Anechiarico/Jacobs, The pursuit of absolute integrity, op. cit., p. 16.

279 Mark D. Jarvis/Paul G. Thomas, The limits of accountability: What can and cannot be accomplished in the dialectics of accountability?' Paper presented at Dalhousie University, Halifax, November 11-13, 2009.

280 Demmke et al., Regulating conflicts of interest for holders of public office in the European Union, op. cit.

Overall, the Member States dispose over a variety of ethics instruments:

- Rules, Standards, Codes;
- Value Management;
- Ethical Leadership;
- Whistle-blowing;
- Disciplinary rules;
- Job Rotation;
- Risk Analysis of vulnerable positions;
- Training and Dilemma Training;
- Integrity Plans;
- Scandal Management;
- Audits;
- Integrity Officers;
- Registers of Interest;
- Transparency requirements;
- Internet based self-assessments;
- Ethics climate survey;
- Awareness raising instruments.

Each instrument and policy must be seen in different political, economical, cultural and institutional contexts. For example, the role and effects of whistle-blowing differ from country to country and from institution to institution. The same applies to gift policies. Whereas in some countries strict gift-policies may be highly effective and also easy to implement, this is not the case in other countries where zero-gift policies would be in conflict with local values.

Many other issues cannot be easily evaluated as to their effectiveness. For example, the effective institutionalisation of ethics, the effects of educational instruments, the right choice of incentives, the need for severe sanctions but also the nature of HR policies (e.g., the level of salaries) and the internal communication on ethics policies simply depend on too many cultural and organisational factors. Despite these limitations, it is possible to identify a number of policies and instruments and their effects. We follow the typology developed by Hesse et al.[281] and identify nine possible effects of ethics policies and instruments (see Table 21 on page 152).

---

281 Joachim Hesse/Christopher Hood/Guy Peters (Eds.), Paradoxes in public sector reform: An international comparison, op. cit.

Table 21. Assessment of effects of ethics policies and instruments

	Impact on other goals		
Impact	**None** (no side-effects)	**Positive side-effects**	**Negative side-effects**
Positively effective main goal achieved	Continuous awareness raising; ethical leadership; ethical culture; distributional, procedural and interactional justice; existence of clear targets, objectives, plans in the field of ethics policies; coherent instruments; commitment to high standards; knowledge on rules and standards	Media attention	Transparency requirements and intrusion in privacy; reporting of financial interests and intrusion in privacy; monitoring of registers of interest and red tape; post-employment rules and obstacles to mobility; costs for monitoring; training and institutionalisation of ethics increase in rules, standards and awareness more violation of rules; ethics abused for political interests
Ineffective no effect	Ethics principles and codes (if not taken seriously); oath; poor implementation and enforcement of ethics policies	Self-assessments and awareness; ethics climate surveys	
Negatively effective reverse effects	Ethics abused as political instrument	Media attention	Ethics misused for religious purposes and moral politics; torture as ethical instrument; distributional, procedural and interactional injustice; unethical leadership

For example, some instruments are relatively ineffective (so far post-employment policies as many Member States have suggested in our study), others are evaluated more positively (for example, ethics training). In fact, most ethics instruments and policies seem to have positive effects but also some negative side-effects. Ethics instruments and policies with clear positive or negative effects are always of a more general nature (for example, continuous awareness raising, torture used as means to maximise utility)[282]. Although we believe that the role of the media and transparency have positive effects, both can also have negative side-effects if ethics policies are becoming entirely scandal-driven policies and being abused for political and media purposes. Notwithstanding the differences between countries, they share a central characteristic: ethics have become ever more scandal-driven which means that decision-makers largely react to the media attention.

One should also distinguish between ethics instruments that have the potential to be much more effective and others that have proven over longer periods of time that they have a rather limited impact. In our study, leadership is considered to be the most effective instrument in the fight against corruption and unethical behaviour. However, in practice, leadership is also considered one of the most important obstacles for an effective policy. The case of leadership shows that ethics policies can have various effects. These effects may even change over time and are related to individuals and personality.

As van den Heuvel et al. show, often instruments are perceived as more effective when they are existing, known and applied in the administration. For example, newer soft instruments are often considered to be less effective simply because they are also less known. The authors also argue that the perception as regards the effectiveness of an instrument increases if the instrument is applied in practice. For example, if ethics training is offered it is also considered to be more effective. If a risk analysis is carried out its effectiveness is considered to be much higher as if the effectiveness of this instrument is only considered in theory[283].

One should also mention that judgments whether instruments are considered to be more or less effective depend very much on the group of respondents and organisational culture. For example, politicians judge the effectiveness of instruments differently than administrators, and a police administration may have a different perspective than the Ministry of Social Affairs.

---

282 Lying is used frequently in politics as well as in administrative practices, but, as such, it has many different effects. Therefore, we refrain from inserting lying as an instrument in our assessment of potential effects of ethics instruments.

283 Van den Heuvel et al., Integriteit van het lokaal bestuur, op. cit., pp. 75, 96-97.

Studying the effectiveness of ethics policies cannot be done without a deep understanding of reform policies, management reforms and their effects on ethics. Our study shows that modern public management reforms have contradictory effects in the field of ethics and on the behaviour of public officials. Today, administrative reform dynamics produce less and more ethical challenges at the same time, but in different policies and HR areas and as regards different instruments. The field of mobility policies is just one example. Whereas more Member States promote and support more mobility between the public and the private sector (and remove legal, political and technical obstacles to switch sides), they are becoming increasingly aware about the ethical consequences: potentially more conflicts of interest, new value dilemmas, threats to the classical public service ethos and the need to regulate new post-employment issues.

In the future, it will be an important task to further define the effects of different instruments and polices in different contexts. Only then will it be possible to further progress as regards the question whether or not ethics policies and instruments are effective, or not. Therefore, we recommend to continue work on the above mentioned theoretical framework as it allows for a fine-tuned analysis as regards the effectiveness of different instruments in different contexts. Applying this concept to the field of ethics may also help to bring in a more rational, non-ideological discourse.

Still, as already stated above, this study is no plea for removing ethics policies. Although more rules and standards are no guarantee of more effectiveness, abolishing rules could easily raise public and media suspicion and contribute to lower levels of public trust. Despite the fact that some Member States are sceptical as to the effectiveness of post-employment rules, we believe that more should be done in this area. However, taking into consideration the issue of effectiveness remains a priority. For example, how can we design effective and deterrent post-employment rules in times of increasing fixed-terms contracts? Will talented people, experts, advisors or politicians be deterred from entering public or private sector jobs if tough and strict revolving door rules will be implemented? On the other hand, blurring boundaries between the public and private sector require innovative solutions to public/private sector switchers.

Answers as to the effects of austerity measures and the financial crisis on workplace ethics are still premature. However, there are enough reasons to be concerned: those Member States which are struggling with economic and financial difficulties agree that the effects of austerity measures affect negatively the workplace behaviour. Or as Anechiarico and Jabobs put it: "In short, if public employees are treated like second-or third-class citizens, they will act accordingly, and no amount of laws or controls will remedy the situation. In some cases, they will make things worse. Poorly paid, poorly treated public employees will be alienated and demoralized"[284].Under such circumstances unethical behaviour is easily rationalised.

So far, developments within the political and administrative systems have not expanded the meaning and the practical expression of the concept of ethics. Today, governments invest more resources in ethics policies than ever before. In many cases governments have institutionalised weak and fragmented ethics infrastructures as a reaction to political scandals in a rather ad-hoc, hasty and fragmented way. A new ethics bureaucracy is most likely emerging in the field of conflicts of interest (especially financial disclosure policies).

Overall, the institutionalisation of ethics policies seems to be the weakest point of all. Therefore, concerns about rising costs and the emergence of an ethics bureaucracy are rather limited. Most ethics structures (audit policies, monitoring programmes and ethics committees) are not independent. Instead, they strongly depend on the influence of the political class. Most questions remain as to the effects of management and the monitoring of registers and disclosure policies. So far, many Member States shy away from strengthening independent institutional structures. Also important advisory and awareness raising bodies, like BIOS in the Netherlands, remain an exception. However, we are cautious to recommend best practices as administrative traditions, structures, cultures and challenges are too different.

Nevertheless, the weak institutionalisation of ethics policies confirms another hypothesis: ethics policies focus presently on the input rather than on the output. Therefore, governments should move their focus from decision-making to implementation and enforcement of ethics policies. The latter should be further strengthened. Whereas ethical values and principles receive more and more attention in the media and on the political level, our findings also show that the implementation of ethics policies is not taken seriously. This discrepancy between input and output can also be seen as regards individual instruments: whereas some issues which are seen as important, popular and fashionable receive an ongoing attention, for example the whole field of conflicts of interests, other issues do not receive much attention.

As it seems, ethical requirements imposed onto public officials will continue to increase, and the meaning of ethics will further widen over the years to come. Despite the complex link between public management reforms and ethics, public

---

284 Anecharico/Jacobs, The pursuit of absolute integrity, op. cit., p. 202.

officials will not only be required to avoid ethical misconduct. Instead, they shall avoid even the appearance of unethical conduct as this is feared to undermine public trust. At least for public officials and Holders of Public Officials, ethics will not always be a win-win policy in the future.

Similarly to Pollitt and Bouckaert in the field of public management reforms in Europe[285], we remain cautious about what can be achieved and how it can be done in the field of ethics and good governance. Understanding what is and what is not possible should be valuable knowledge. Despite this caution, we hope that this study provides plenty of evidence of successful and less change. We strongly believe that good governance and public-service ethics make a big difference to the effects and the legitimacy of the national public services.

---

285 Christopher Pollitt/Geert Bouckaert, Public management reform: A comparative analysis, third edition, Oxford, 2011, p. 182.

LITERATURE

T. W. Adorno/E. Frenkel-Brunswik/D. J. Levinson/R.N. Sanford, The authoritarian personality, New York, Harper and Row, 1950.

Sam Agere, Promoting good governance: Principles, practices and perspectives. Commonwealth Secretariat, 2000.

Pablo Alonso/Gregory Lewis, Public service motivation and job performance: Evidence from the federal sector, in: American Review of Public Administration, Vol. 31, No. 4/2001, pp. 363-380.

Jens Chr. Andvig/Odd-Helge Fjeldstad (Eds.), Research on corruption: A policy oriented survey, Chr. Michelsen Institute (CMI) & Norwegian Institute of International Affairs (NUPI), Bergen/Oslo 2000.

Frank Anechiarico/Leo Huberts/Frederique Six, Local integrity systems: World cities fighting corruption and safeguarding integrity, Boom, Amsterdam, 2008.

Frank Anechiarico/James B. Jacobs, The pursuit of absolute integrity, Chicago and London, 1996.

Kwame Anthony Appiah, Eine Frage der Ehre oder Wie es moralischen Revolution kommt. C.H.Beck, Munchen, 2011.

APSA, A guide to professional ethics in political science, American Political Science Association, second edition, revised 2008, http://www.apsanet.org/media/PDFs/ethicsguideweb.pdf, last time checked on 26.3.2012.

Aristotle, Nicomachean ethics, in: Britanica Great Books, Vol. 9.

Joseph L. Badaracco/Richard Ellsworth, Leadership and quest for integrity, Harvard Business School, Harvard, 1993.

Zygmunt Bauman, Dialektik der Ordnung – Die Moderne und der Holocaust, Europäische Verlagsanstalt, Hamburg, 2000.

Nathalie Behnke, Ethics as apple pie: The arms race of ethical standards in congressional and presidential campaigns. Paper presented at the EGPA conference on Ethics and Integrity of Governance: A transatlantic dialogue in Leuven in June 2005.

Nathalie Behnke, Monitoring public administrators or signalling trustworthiness to the demos? The two functions of ethics regulations, in: Polis 61, University of Hagen, 2006.

Hans A.G.M. Bekke/Frits M. van der Meer, Civil service systems in Western Europe, Edward Elgar Publishing Ltd, 2000.

J. Bernerth/Jack Walker/F. Walter/RR. Hirschfeld, A study of workplace justice. Differences during times of change: It is not all about me, in: The Journal of Applied Behavioural Science, Vol. 47, No. 3/2011, pp. 336-359.

John Raymond Boatright, Ethics and the conduct of business, Prentice Hall, 2008.

Danielle Bossaert/Christoph Demmke, Main challenges in the field of ethics and integrity in the EU Member States, EIPA, Maastricht, 2005.

Mark Bovens, Het ongelijk van Dales. Bestuurskunde, Vol. 15, No. 1/2006, pp. 64-74.

Mark Bovens/A. Wille, Waar bleef het vertrouwen in de overheid? Bestuurskunde, Vol. 15, No. 4/2006, pp. 50-64.

Barry Bozeman, Bureaucracy and red tape, Prentice Hall, New Jersey, 2000.

Marc Bovens/Anton Hemerijck, Het verhaal van de moraal: Een empirisch onderzoek naar de sociale bedding van morele bindingen, Boom, 1996.

Gene A. Brewer/Sally Colman Selden/Rex L. Facer II, Individual conceptions of public service motivation, in: Public Administration Review, Vol. 60, No. 3/2000, pp. 254-264.

Lynelle Briggs, Testing APS ethics: Where's the integrity?, in: The Australian Journal of Public Administration, Vol. 68, No. 2/2009.

David Brin, The transparent society, Perseus Books, Cambridge M.A., 1998.

British House of Commons, The public service ethos, Seventh Report of the Public Administration Committee, 13 June 2002.

Michael E. Brown/Linda K. Trevino, Ethical leadership: A review and future directions, In: The Leadership Quarterly, Vol. 17, 2006, pp. 595-616.

Gerard Carney, Conflict of interest: Legislators, ministers and public officials, Transparency International Working Paper, 1998.

Antonio Bar Cendon (Ed.), Accountability in public administration: reconciling democracy, efficiency and ethics, Brussels, IIAS, 2000.

J. D. Coggburn, The benefits of human resource centralization: Insights from a survey of human resource directors in a decentralized state, in: Public Administration Review, Vol. 65, No. 4/2005, pp. 424-435.

Yochi Cohen-Charasha/Paul E. Spector, The role of justice in organizations: A meta-analysis, in: Organizational Behavior and Human Decision Processes, Vol. 86, No. 2/2001, pp. 278–321;

Terry L. Cooper, The responsible administrator, Jossey Bass, 5th edition, 2006.

Council of State, Public report of the Council of State, studies and documents, reflections on the civil service, Paris, 2003.

Russel Cropanzano/Jorgan H. Stein/Thierry Nadisc, Social Justice and the experience of emotion, Routledge, New York, 2011.

David Dagan, Personal politics: All too often legislators' private interests are hidden from private view. Special report, 24 September 2004, Center of Public Integrity, 2004.

James B. DeConinck, The effect of organizational justice, perceived organizational support, and perceived supervisor support on marketing employees' level of trust, in: Journal of Business Research, Vol. 63, No. 12/2010, pp. 1349–1355.

Paul Dekker/Joep de Hart/Paul de Beer/Christa Hubers, De moraal in de publieke opinie (Morals in Public Opinion), Social and Cultural Planning Agency (Sociaal en Cultureel Planbureau), The Hague, 2004, http://www.scp.nl, last time checked on 26.3.2012.

Christoph Demmke, Ethik und Integrität in den öffentlichen Diensten in Europa. Journal for Public and Nonprofit Services, Vol. 29, No. 1/2006, pp. 68-84.

Christoph Demmke, Are civil servants different because they are civil servants? European Institute of Public Administration, Maastricht, 2006.

Christoph Demmke/Gerhard Hammerschmid/Renate E. Meyer, Decentralisation and accountability as a focus of public administration modernisation: Challenges and consequences for human resource management, European Institute of Public Administration, Maastricht/Brussels, 2006.

Christoph Demmke/Mark Bovens/Thomas Henökl/Timo Moilanen, Regulating conflicts of interest for holders of public office in the European Union, EIPA, Maastricht, 2008.

Christoph Demmke/Thomas Henökl/Timo Moilanen, What are public services good at? Success of public services in the field of human resource management, Report to the 50th Meeting of the Directors-General of Public Services of the Member States of the European Union, May 2008.

Christoph Demmke, Leistungsbezahlung in den öffentlichen Diensten der EU-Staaten, Der moderne Staat, Vol. 2, No. 1/2009, pp. 53-73.

Christoph Demmke/Timo Moilanen, Civil services in the EU of 27, Peter Lang, Frankfurt/M., 2010.

Georg Dench (Ed.), The rise and rise of meritocracy, Blackwell, Oxford, 2006.

W.N. Dunn, Public policy analysis: An introduction, Fourth Edition, Upper Saddle River, NJ: Pearson/Prentice Hall, 2008.

Emile Durkheim, The division of labour in society, Free Press, 1997.

John S. Dryzek/Bonnie Honig/Anne Philips (Eds.), The Oxford handbook of political theory, Oxford University Press, New York, 2006.

Alain Ehrenberg, La societe du malaise, Odile Jacob, 2010.

Yves Emery/Carole Wyser, Identities of public sector employees as a source of inspiration for differentiating HRM practices: The Swiss case, Paper presented at the EGPA Conference, 2-5 September 2009.

Ethik im öffentlichen Dienst, Report of the Parliament's administrative supervisory authority for the attention of the Audit Committee of the National Council of 30 October 1998.

EUPAN, Main features of an ethics framework for the public sector. Proposed by the Dutch EU Presidency and adopted by the Directors General responsible for Public Administration in the Members States and the institutions of the European Union in their 43rd meeting in Maastricht. It has been published in

Danielle Bossaert/Christoph Demmke, Main challenges in the field of ethics and integrity in the EU Member States, EIPA, Maastricht, 2005.

European Foundation for the Improvement of Living and Working Conditions, Effect of performance-related bonuses on gender pay gap, Dublin, 2008.

Herbert Fain, The case for a zero gift policy, in: Public Integrity, Vol. 4, No. 1/2002, pp. 61-80.

M.A Feldheim/ X.Wang, Ethics and public trust, in: Public Integrity, 2003-2004, Vol. 6, No. 1/2004, pp. 63-75.

Cyrille Fijnaut/Leo Huberts, Corruption, integrity and law enforcement, Kluwer Law International, 2002.

J. Fleming/Ian Holland, Motivating ethical conduct in government ministers. Paper presented at the International Institute for Public Ethics, Ottawa, September 2000.

Mark S. Frankel, Professional codes, why, how and with what impact?, in: Journal of Business Ethics, Vol. 8, Numbers 2-3/1989, pp. 109-115.

George H. Frederickson, The spirit of public administration, San Francisco, Jossey-Bass, 1997.

George H. Frederickson/Richard K. Ghere (Eds.), Ethics in public management, Sharpe, New York, 2005.

Suzy Fox/Paul E. Spector (Eds.), Counterproductive work behaviour, Washington D.C., 2005.

M. Gaugler, Bundestagsabgeordnete zwischen Mandat und Aufsichtsrat, VDM, Saarbrücken, 2006.

Edgar Norman Gladden, Civil services of the United Kingdom 1856-1970, Frank Cass, London, 1967.

Edgar Norman Gladden, A history of public administration, Vol. II, Frank Cass, London, 1972.

Eleanor Glor, Codes of conduct and generations of public servants, in: International Review of Administrative Sciences, Vol. 67, 2001, pp. 525-541.

Gjalf de Graaf/Zeger van der Wal, On value differences experienced by sector switchers, in: Administration and Society, Vol. 40, No.1/ 2008, pp.79-103.
Jerald Greenberg, Insidious workplace behaviour, Routledge, 2010.
Amy Gutmann/Dennis Thompson, Ethics and politics, Thomson/Wadsworth, Fourth Edition, 2006.

Gerhard Hammerschmid/Renate E. Meyer/Isabel Egger-Peitler, Das Konzept der Public Service Motivation – Status Quo der internationalen Diskussion und erste empirische Evidenzen für den deutschsprachigen Raum, in: Der moderne Staat, Zeitschrift für Public Policy, Recht und Management Heft 1/2009, pp. 73-92.

Gottfried Hegel, Elements of the Philosophy of Right, Cambridge University Edition, 1991.

Jonny Hellgren/Markus Sverke/Kerstin Isaksson, A two-dimensional approach to job insecurity: Consequences for employees attitudes and well-being, in: European Journal of Work and Organisational Psychology, Vol. 8, 1999, pp. 179-195.

Joachim Hesse/Christopher Hood/Guy Peters (Eds.), Paradoxes in public sector reform: An international comparison, Duncker & Humblot, Berlin 2003.

Leo Hickman, A life stripped bare. My year trying to live ethically, Eden, 2006.

Alain Hoekstra/Leo Kaptein/D. van de Burg, Het institutionaliseren van integriteit: De organisatie van de integriteitsfunctie binnen lokale overheden verkend, in: Bestuurswetenschappen, No. 5/2010, pp. 54-73.

Geert Hofstede, Culture's consequences – comparing values, behaviors, institutions and organizations across nations, second edition, Thousand Oaks, London, New Delhi, 2001.

Christopher Hood/David Heald (Eds.), Transparency. The key to better governance? Oxford University Press, 2006.

A. Hoogerwerf & M. Herweijer, Overheidsbeleid: Een inleiding in de beleidswetenschap, Kluwer, Alphen aan den Rijn, 2008.

David Houston, Public service motivation: A multivariate test, in: Journal of Public Administration Research and Theory, Vol. 10, No. 4/2000, pp. 713-727.

Anne P. Hubbell/Rebecca M. Chory-Assad, Motivating factors: Perceptions of justice and their relationship with managerial and organizational trust, in: Communication Studies, Vol. 56, No. 1/2005, pp. 47-70.

Leo W. J. Huberts, What can be done against public corruption and fraud? Expert views on strategies to protect public integrity, in: Crime, Law & Social Change, Vol. 29, No. 2-3/1998, pp. 209-224.

Leo W. J. Huberts/Jeroen Maesschalck/Carole Jurkiewicz, Ethics and integrity of governance: Perspectives across frontiers, Edward Elgar, Massachusetts, 2008.

Leo W. J. Huberts/J.H.J. van den Heuvel (Eds.), Integrity at the public-private interface, Shaker, Maastricht, 1999.

Independent Commission against Corruption and Crime, Managing public ethics in the public sector, Guidelines, Australia, Sydney 2004.

Mark D. Jarvis/Paul G. Thomas, The limits of accountability: What can and cannot be accomplished in the dialectics of accountability?' Paper presented at Dalhousie University, Halifax, November 11-13, 2009.

Immanuel Kant, Metaphysic of morals, in: Britannica Great Books, Vol. 42.

Joy H. Karriker/Margaret L. Williams, Organizational justice and organizational citizenship behavior: A mediated multifoci model, in: Journal of Management, Vol. 35, No. 1/2009, pp. 112-135.

Michael Kelly (Ed.), Openness and transparency in governance, European Institute of Public Administration, Maastrict, 2000

Seok Eun Kim/Dian Rubianty, Perceived fairness of performance appraisals in the federal government: Does it matter?, in: Review of Public Personnel Administration, Vol. 31, No. 4/2011, pp. 329-349.

JJ. Kish-Gephart/D.A Harrison/L.K. Treviño (2010), Bad apples, bad cases, and bad barrels: Meta-analytic evidence about sources of unethical decisions at work, in: Journal of Applied Psychology, Vol. 95, No. 1/2010, pp. 1-31.

Bert Klandermans/Tinka van Vuuren, Job insecurity: Introduction, in: European Journal of Work and Organisational Psychology, Vol. 8, 1999, pp. 145-153.

Emile Kolthoff, Ethics and new public management. Empirical research into the effects of businesslike government on ethics and integrity, Boom Juridische Uitgevers, 2007.

Anne Käßner, Nebentätigkeiten und Nebeneinkünfte der Mitglieder des Deutschen Bundestages, Duncker und Humblot, Berlin, 2010.

Karin Lasthuizen, Leading to integrity: Empirical research into the effects of leadership on ethics and integrity, Enschede, Printpartners Ipskamp, 2008.

Alain Lawton, Developing and implementing codes of ethics, paper presented at the EGPA Annual Conference, Lisbon 3rd- 6th September 2003.

Alan Lawton/Alan Doig, Researching ethics for public service organizations: The view from Europe, in: Public Integrity, Vol. 8, 1/2006, pp. 11-33.

Carol W. Lewis/Stuart C. Gilman, The ethics challenge in public service: A problem-solving guide, Jossey-Bass, second edition, 2005.

Niklas Luhmann, Die Moral der Gesellschaft, Suhrkamp, Frankfurt/M., 2008.

Steven Lukes, Moral relativism, Picador, New York, 2008.

G. S. Mackenzie, Scandal proof: Do ethics laws make government better? Brookings Institution, Washington D.C, 2002.

Siegfried Magiera/Karl-Peter Sommermann/Jacques Ziller (Eds.), Verwaltungswissenschaft und Verwaltungspraxis in nationaler und transnationaler Perspektive, Dunker und Humblot, Berlin, 2008.

M. Maguire, Ethics in the public service - current issues and practice, paper presented at the EGPA Annual Conference in Leuven in 1997.

Patrick Maravic/Christoph Reichard, New public management and corruption: IPMN dialogue and analysis, International Public Management Review, Vol. 4, No. 1/2003, pp. 84-129.

Patrick Maravic, Public management reform and corruption – conceptualizing the unintended consequences, in: Administratie si Management Public, No. 8/2007, pp. 126-143.

Mark J. Martinko/Michael Gundlach/Scott Douglas, Towards an integrative theory of counterproductive workplace behavior: A casual reasoning perspective, in: International Journal of Selection and Assessment, No. 1-2/2002, pp. 36-50.

John J. Mearsheimer, Why leaders lie: The truth about lying in international politics, Oxford University Press, New York, 2011.

Donald Menzel, Research on ethics and integrity in governance: A review and assessment, in: Public Integrity, Vol. 7, No. 2/2005, pp. 147–168.

Donald Menzel, Ethics moments in government, CRC Press, Boca Raton, 2010.

Donald Menzel/Harvey L. White (Eds.), The state of public administration, Sharpe, London, 2011.

Robert K. Merton, Social structure and anomie, in: American Sociological Review, Vol. 3, No. 5/1938, pp. 672-682.

Ministerie van Binnenlandse Zaken en Koningsrijkrelaties, Integriteit van de Overheid, Den Hague, 2007.

Henry Mintzberg, Managing, San Francisco, 2009.

Timo Moilanen/Ari Salminen, Comparative study on the public-service ethics of the EU Member States, Edita Prima Plc, Helsinki, 2007.

S. Muhle (2006), Mehr Transparenz bei Nebeneinkünften von Abgeordneten? Zur Weiterentwicklung des Abgeordnetenrechts in Niedersachsen, in: Zeitschrift für Parlamentsfragen, No. 2/2006, p. 266-276.

National Defence of Canada, Fundamentals of Canadian defence ethics, defence ethics program, January 2002.

Stafford Northcote/C. E. Trevelyan, The organisation of the permanent civil service, Parliamentary Papers, Volume XXVII, 1854.

OECD, Ethics in the public service, current issues and practices, Public Management Occasional Papers, No. 14, 1996.

OECD, Managing government ethics, Puma Policy Brief No. 1, Paris 1997.

OECD, Trust in government: Ethics measures in OECD countries, Paris 2000.

OECD, Building public trust: Ethics measures in OECD countries, Puma Policy Brief No.7, Spring 2000.

OECD, Public sector integrity: A framework for assessment, Paris 2005.
OECD, Growing unequal?, Paris, 2008.

OECD, Towards a sound integrity framework: Instruments, processes, structures, and conditions for implementation. Global Forum on Public Governance, Paris, 4-5 May 2009.

OECD, The right to open public administrations in Europe, SIGMA paper no. 46, Paris 2010.

OECD, Government at a glance, Paris 2011.

OECD, Divided we stand: Why inequality keeps rising? Paris 2011.

Lynn Sharp Paine, Managing for organizational integrity, Harvard Business Review, 1994.

Matthias Pechstein/Rudolf Summer, Beiträge zum Beamtenrecht, Tuebingen, 2007.

James Perry, Measuring public service motivation: An assessment of construct reliability and validity, in: Journal of Public Administration Research and Theory, Vol. 6, No. 1/1996. pp. 5-22.

James Perry/Annie Hondeghem (Eds.), Motivation in public management, Oxford 2008.

Guy Peters/Jon Pierre, Handbook of public administration, Sage, 2003.

Christopher Pollitt/Geert Bouckaert, Public management reform: A comparative analysis, third edition, Oxford, 2011.

Karl Popper, Objective knowledge, Oxford University Press, 1972

R. D. Putnam, Making democracy work: Civil traditions in modern Italy, Princeton, 1993.

Hal G. Rainey, Understanding and managing public organistions, third edition, Jossey Bass, San Francisco, 2003.

James E Rauch/Peter B. Evans, Bureaucratic structure and bureaucratic performance in less developed countries, in: Journal of Public Economics, Vol. 75, No. 1/2000, pp. 49-71.
John Rawls, A theory of justice, Harvard University Press, 1971.

Martin Rhodes/Paul Heywood/Vincent Wright (Eds.), Developments in West European politics, Basingstoke 1997.

Stephen Robbins, Essentials of organisational behaviour. Pearson/Prentice Hall, 2005.

John Rohr, To run a constitution, the legitimacy of the administrative state, University Press of Kansas, 1986.

Denis Saint-Martin/Fred Thompson (Eds.), Public ethics and governance: Standards and practices in comparative perspective. Vol. 14. Amsterdam/Boston/Heidelberg//New York/ Oxford/Paris/San Diego/San Francisco/Singapore/Sydney/Tokyo, 2006.

Denis Saint-Martin, Should the federal ethics counsellor become an independent officer of parliament?, in: Canadian Public Policy, Analyse de Politiques, Vol. XXiX, No. 2/2003.

Ari Salminen (Ed.), Ethical governance, University of Vaasa, 2010.

A. de Schrijver/K. Delbeke/J. Maesschalck/S. Pleysier, Fairness perceptions and organisational misbehaviour: An empirical study, The American Review of Public Administration, Vol. 40, No. 6/2010, pp. 691-703.

Marshall Schmink (Ed.), Managerial ethics, Routledge, New York, 2010.

Hagen Schulze, Staat und Nation in der europäischen Geschichte, Beck, 2004.

Gerhard Schulze, Die Sünde, Carl Hanser, München, 2006.

Robert Schwartz, Breaches of integrity and accountability institutions: Auditors, anti-corruption agencies and commissions of inquiry. Paper presented at the meeting of the Study Group on Ethics and Integrity of Governance, Annual Conference of the European Group of Public Administration, September 2003, Oeiras, Portugal.

Martin Seel, 111 Tugenden, 111 Laster, Fischer, Frankfurt/Main, 2011.

Jay M. Shafritz/Albert C. Hyde, Classics of public administration, The Dorsey Press, Chicago, Illinois, Second Edition, 1987.

Jay M. Shafritz/Albert C. Hyde, Classics of public administration, Sixth Edition, Boston, 2008.

Standards in Public Office Commission, Guidelines on compliance with the provisions of the ethics in public office acts, 1995 and 2001, Dublin, January 2003.

Andrew Stark, Conflict of interest in American public life, Harvard, Cambridge, 2000.

David Tarren, Improving trust in central government, A report for TUNED and EUPAN, 2009.

Dennis F. Thompson, Restoring responsibility: Ethics in government, business, and healthcare. Cambridge University Press, 2004.

Dennis F. Thompson, Overcoming the conflict of interest in congressional ethics. Paper for the panel on Congressional Ethics Enforcement, Woodrow Wilson International Center, Washington, D.C., January 16, 2007.

Transparency International, Global corruption report 2003, http://www.transparency.org/publications/gcr/gcr_2003#download, last time checked on 26.3.2012.

Patrick von Maravic, Decentralised corruption in Germany, in: Public Administration Quarterly, Vol. 30, No. 3-4/2007, pp. 440-478.

Dwight Waldo, The administrative state, Ronald Press, New York, 1948.

Christian Waldhoff, Das missverstandene Mandat: Verfassungsrechtliche Maßstäbe zur Normierung der erweiterten Offenbarungspflichten der Abgeordneten des Deutschen Bundestages, in: Zeitschrift für Parlamentsfragen, No. 2/2006, p. 251-266.

Michael Walzer, Sphären der Gerechtigkeit, Ein Plädoyer für Pluralität und Gleichheit, Frankfurt/New York, 2006.
J.H.J. van den Heuvel/Leo Huberts/Zeger van der Wal/K. Steenburgen, Integriteit van het lokaal bestuur, Boom, 2010.

Zeger van der Wal, Value solidity, differences, similarities and conflicts between the organisational values of government and business, Dissertation at the Free University of Amsterdam, 2008.

Zeger van der Wal/E. Th. van Hout, Is public value pluralism paramount? The intrinsic multiplicity and hybridity of public values, in: International Journal of Public Administration, Vol. 32, 3-4/2009, pp. 220-231.

Steven van de Walle, Perceptions of administrative performance: The key to trust in government? Dissertation, University of Leuven, No. 79, 2004.

Steven van de Walle/S. van Roosbroek/Geert Bouckaert, Trust in the public sector: Is there any evidence for a long-term decline?, in: International Review of Administrative Sciences, Vol. 74, No. 1/2008, pp. 215-216.

Sandra van Thiel/Zeger van der Wal, Birds of a feather? The effect of organisational value congruence on the relationship between ministries and quangos, in: Public Organisation Review, Vol. 10 No 4/2010, pp. 377-397.

Caroline van Rijckhem/Beatrice Weder, Corruption and the rate of temptation: Do low wages in the civil service cause corruption, Working Paper WP 97/73, International Monetary Fund, Washington D.C. 1997.

Montgomery van Wart, Codes of ethics as living documents, Public Integrity, Vol. 5 No. 4/2003, pp. 331-346.

M. E. Warren, Democracy and deceit: Regulating appearances of corruption, in: American Journal of Political Science, Vol. 50, No. 1/2006, pp. 162-174.

Max Weber, Politik als Beruf, Reclam, Stuttgart 1999.

Max Weber, The protestant ethic and the spirit of capitalism, Penguin Books, 2002.

Max Weber, Wirtschaft und Gesellschaft, Volmedia, Paderborn, 1922.

Wetenschappelijke Raad voor het Regeringsbeleid WRR (Scientific Council for Government Policy), Waarden, normen en de last van het gedrag (Values, standards and the burden of behaviour), The Hague, 2003.

Hans de Witte, Job insecurity and psychological well-being: Review of the literature and exploration of some unresolved issues, in: European Journal of Work and Organisational Psychology, Vol. 8, 1999, pp. 155-177.
Hans Herbert von Arnim, Der gekaufte Abgeordnete – Nebeneinkünfte und Korruptionsproblematik, in: Neue Zeitschrift für Verwaltungsrecht, No. 3/2006 pp. 249-254
World Bank, Anticorruption in transition: A contribution to the policy debate, Washington, 2000.

World Bank Institute, Proactive transparency: The future of the right to information? Washington D.C., 2011.

Philip Zimbardo, The Lucifer effect: Understanding how good people turn evil, Random House Trade Paperbacks, 2008.

P. Zoghbi-Manrique-de-Lara, Do unfair procedures predict employees ethical behavior by deactivating formal regulations? in: Journal of Business Ethics, Vol. 94, No. 3/2010, pp. 411-425.

United Nations Economic and Social Commission for Asia and the Pacific, What is good governance? http://www.unescap.org/pdd/prs/ProjectActivities/Ongoing/gg/governance.asp, last time checked on 26.3.2012.

ANNEX: SURVEY QUESTIONNAIRE

Questionnaire - some additional questions to the policy paper

On the following pages you will find a supplementary questionnaire that consists of seven themes split into sub-questions. Though replies to the questions are necessarily subjective in nature, they should to the extent possible reflect a broad view within your administration. Please mark your options and write comments in this e-document. If you have technical difficulties in filling out this document, we can send you the questionnaire in the file format of your choice.

Please reply by filling out this questionnaire and sending it to Mr. Christoph Demmke at c.demmke@eipa.eu and Mr. Timo Moilanen by e-mail at t.moilanen@eipa.eu **by the 9th of September 2011** at the latest. You may answer in English, French or German.

A first discussion around the issue will take place on 12-13 September in the first Human Resource Working Group meeting in Warsaw. The preliminary findings will be presented at the second Human Resource Working Group meeting in Cracow 17-18.11.2011 and the final report will be presented at the Director-General meeting in Warsaw 12-13.12.2011.

Thank you in advance for your co-operation and valuable comments.

Contact information

Professor Dr. Christoph Demmke
Unit 2 - European Public Management
European Institute of Public Administration
P.O. Box 1229
NL-6201 BE Maastricht
e-mail: c.demmke@eipa.eu

Seconded National Expert Timo Moilanen
Unit 2 - European Public Management
European Institute of Public Administrat.
P.O. Box 1229
NL-6201 BE Maastricht
e-mail: t.moilanen@eipa.eu
tel. +31 433 296 389 (office)

1. Background information

1.1 Name of the Member State:

1.2 Name and title of the respondent:

1.3 Respondent's organisation:

1.4Respondent's email and telephone information:

2. Public discussions on public-service ethics

2.1 Have the following issues been a subject of public discussion (TV, newspapers) or administrative discussion (professional events and journals) in your country during the last five year?

	Public discussion			Administrative discussion		
	No	Somewhat	Intensive	No	Somewhat	Intensive
a) political corruption	☐	☐	☐	☐	☐	☐
b) administrative corruption	☐	☐	☐	☐	☐	☐
c) misconduct	☐	☐	☐	☐	☐	☐
d) misuse of organisational resources	☐	☐	☐	☐	☐	☐
e) conflict of interest issues related to politicians	☐	☐	☐	☐	☐	☐
f) conflict of interest issues related to civil servants	☐	☐	☐	☐	☐	☐
g) post-employment issues related to politicians	☐	☐	☐	☐	☐	☐
h) post-employment issues related to civil servants	☐	☐	☐	☐	☐	☐
i) discrimination	☐	☐	☐	☐	☐	☐
j) mobbing	☐	☐	☐	☐	☐	☐
k) core values (e.g. openness)	☐	☐	☐	☐	☐	☐
l) ethical standards	☐	☐	☐	☐	☐	☐
m) unethical behaviour in general (please comment)	☐	☐	☐	☐	☐	☐
n) other ethical issues (please write a comment)	☐	☐	☐	☐	☐	☐

Comments:

2.2 Are the above-mentioned discussions in your country characterised mostly by

scandal-driven debates (concrete problem cases)	☐	☐	☐	☐	☐	value-driven debates (general discussions on values and standards)

Comments:

2.3 Have the discussions led to any responses or practical outcomes? E.g., moral panic leading to more detailed and stricter rules, consensus on new standards of behaviour, new code of conduct, new legal rules, etc.

Comments:

2.4 Have the current public discussions affected the levels of public trust?

Increased trust				Decreased trust	
☐	☐	☐	☐	☐	towards elected officials (politicians)
☐	☐	☐	☐	☐	towards appointed officials (civil servants)

Comments:

2.5 Has the public trust changed during the last years? Which things have contributed to the change / stability?

Comments:

2.6 Do you agree that throughout the last years – within your administration – more issues have been defined as subjects for potential unethical behaviour? (See Chapter 7 for a list of issues considered unethical)

☐ Very much ☐ Somewhat ☐ No changes ☐ Decreased ☐ Cannot say

Comments:

3. Official ethics

3.1 A previous study conducted during the Finnish EU Presidency found out that most EU Member States had introduced a values statement or a code of conduct (Moilanen & Salminen 2006). The prior list of codes can be found in the Annex 1. Have you made any revisions to your code during the last five years (see Annex)? Have you introduced new codes? **Please update any new information directly to the Annex 1 on last page.**

Comments:

3.2 Public-service values and standards of good administrative behaviour can be prescribed in various forms. They are typically communicated as legal act(s), values statements and/or detailed behavioural standards. In some cases behavioural standards lack a written form and they are part of the administrative culture (tacit knowledge). In your country, is there in use

In use ←——→ Not in use

☐	☐	☐	detailed ethics-specific legislation[286]
☐	☐	☐	general legislation without specific reference to ethics[287]
☐	☐	☐	code of conduct stating detailed behavioural standards[288]
☐	☐	☐	code of ethics stating general values or principles[289]

Comments:

3.3 Have the above documents been revised during the last five years? What are the major changes? Have revisions generated any discussions inside public administration or among general public? Has the code raised awareness of ethical issues in your country?

Comments:

Please send a copy (or a reference with link) of the relevant new codes to the researchers to the address above.

---

286 Standards of Ethical Conduct for Employees of the Executive Branch, 5 C.F.R. Part 2635 (USA).

287 Parts of Act on the Openness of Government Activities (FI).

288 Main Features of an Ethics Framework for the Public Sector, EUPAN 2004.

289 The Seven Principles of Public Life by the Committee on Standards of Public Life.

3.4 How have you communicated official public-service values and standards (as defined in laws, codes and regulations) to your public servants? Documents on values and standards are

Yes	No	
☐	☐	automatically provided when someone joins the public service
☐	☐	automatically provided when someone takes a position in a different organisation
☐	☐	part of the employment contract/document
☐	☐	part of in-house training
☐	☐	part of external training
☐	☐	part of e-training

Comments:

3.5 In general, how familiar civil servants are with the official public-service values and standards?

Very cognisant ←——→ Not cognisant at all

☐ ☐ ☐ ☐ ☐

Comments:

3.6 Are there any other specific guidelines/requirements within the public service in addition to the general standards applicable to all public servants?

Yes	No	
☐	☐	agency-specific codes of conduct (e.g., all staff working for some public agency)
☐	☐	field-specific codes of conduct (e.g., additional code for officials dealing with taxes or permissions)

Comments:

3.7 Are elected holders of public office such as members of government (ministers) and members of national assembly (parliamentarians) subject to the same ethics code as public servants or do they have different or more specific rules?

Yes	To some extent	No	
☐	☐	☐	Same behavioural standards apply to both elected and appointed officials

Comments:

4. Impact of Reform Policies on Workplace Behaviour

4.1 Due to the financial crisis many Member States are currently in a process of cutting public employment, freezing or reducing salaries, easing employment protection, increasing retirement age and implementing other similar austerity measures. Would you agree that the austerity measures have generally had the following effects in your country?

	Very much	Somewhat	Not at all	Hard to say
a) decrease of trust in the organisation	☐	☐	☐	☐
b) decrease of trust in leadership	☐	☐	☐	☐
c) perception of unfairness compared to how private sector employees are dealt with	☐	☐	☐	☐
d) perception of unfairness compared to how colleagues are dealt with	☐	☐	☐	☐
e) decrease in workplace commitment	☐	☐	☐	☐
f) decline of ethical values	☐	☐	☐	☐
g) lowering of job satisfaction	☐	☐	☐	☐
h) increase in inappropriate use of resources, e.g., theft and fraud	☐	☐	☐	☐
i) unethical behaviour arising from higher stress levels and higher job intensity	☐	☐	☐	☐
j) increase in anger	☐	☐	☐	☐
k) decrease in loyalty	☐	☐	☐	☐
l) greater tendency towards corruption	☐	☐	☐	☐
m) other impact, what (please comment)	☐	☐	☐	☐

Comments:

4.2 Which public sector and HR-reform trends are most vulnerable to integrity violations (e.g., bribing, favouritism, conflict of interest through gifts or outside activities)?

	Very vulnerable ←		→ Not vulnerable	Cannot say
a) generally, the implementation of new austerity measures (reduction of jobs and salaries, promotion opportunities etc.)	☐	☐	☐	☐
b) pay reforms	☐	☐	☐	☐
c) reforms of social security systems	☐	☐	☐	☐
d) reform of job security	☐	☐	☐	☐
e) introduction of new ICT	☐	☐	☐	☐
f) citizen-orientation	☐	☐	☐	☐
g) openness	☐	☐	☐	☐
i) enhancing mobility between public and private sector)	☐	☐	☐	☐
j) organisational reforms (abolishment of hierarchies)	☐	☐	☐	☐
k) decentralisation of HR responsibilities	☐	☐	☐	☐
l) change of organisational culture	☐	☐	☐	☐
m) promotion policies	☐	☐	☐	☐
n) recruitment policies	☐	☐	☐	☐
o) competency management	☐	☐	☐	☐
p) others, what	☐	☐	☐	☐

Comments:

5. Monitoring and Assessing Ethics Policies and Ethics Instruments

5.1 Generally speaking, which instruments do you consider as more effective in the fight against corruption and other unethical behaviour?

Effective ←				→ Ineffective	
☐	☐	☐	☐	☐	Laws and regulations
☐	☐	☐	☐	☐	Codes
☐	☐	☐	☐	☐	Leadership
☐	☐	☐	☐	☐	Training, incl. dilemma training
☐	☐	☐	☐	☐	Openness, transparency
☐	☐	☐	☐	☐	Registration of financial interests
☐	☐	☐	☐	☐	Post-employment rules
☐	☐	☐	☐	☐	Strict gift policies

☐	☐	☐	☐	☐	Integrity officers providing counselling
☐	☐	☐	☐	☐	Protection of whistle-blowers
☐	☐	☐	☐	☐	Others, what

Comments:

5.2 What do you consider as the major obstacles and difficulties for an effective policy in your public service?

Major obstacle	Minor obstacle	Not an obstacle	
☐	☐	☐	Poor quality of existing laws, regulations and codes
☐	☐	☐	Enforcement of codes (if codes exist)
☐	☐	☐	Lack of active leadership and leadership commitment?
☐	☐	☐	Lack of ethics-related training
☐	☐	☐	Organisational culture does not match with ethical standards
☐	☐	☐	HRM policy contradicts with ethical requirements (no independent selection and recruitment procedures, politicized administration, control of diplomas and references, no review list of vulnerable functions, oath, etc.)
☐	☐	☐	HRM policy is not strictly merit-based (exceptions for politicians, top-managers, public employees, minorities, women, disabled persons)
☐	☐	☐	Ethics policies are not taken seriously – not enough awareness and knowledge of ethics rules
☐	☐	☐	No monitoring (registration of ethical violations lacking)
☐	☐	☐	No independent ethics examinations (e.g., through ethics commissions)
☐	☐	☐	Lack of evaluation of violations
☐	☐	☐	Lack of sanctions/deterrence
☐	☐	☐	Ethics policies are not integrated into other policies (e.g. through unfair recruitment, pay, promotion policies)

5.3 Have monitoring, accountability and control structures been intensified (by way of obliging officials to fill in public registers on income and ancillary activities, the setting up of ethics commissions, ethics officers, control and monitoring mechanisms)?

Comments:

5.4 Is disclosure of financial interests required for public officials?

Yes	No	
☐	☐	concerning elected officials (politicians)
☐	☐	concerning top civil servants
☐	☐	concerning other appointed officials (please specify if exists)

Comments:

5.5 If a financial disclosure system is in use, how is the information used, who receives it and what are potential consequences if a conflict is detected?

Comments:

5.6 Are there any specialised bodies in place to investigate misconduct and corruption in public service? Does the body have authority to prosecute?

Comments:

5.7 Is there any institution, unit or committee, whose task is to coordinate and/or manage the implementation of ethics policy? (name, status, staff and other resources)

Comments:

5.8 Some Member States have started to implement scandal management programs in order to be able to better respond to political and administrative scandals. Do you have one? Do you plan to implement one? Is it effective? Please give a link to the programme (if it exists).

Comments:

5.9 Are more rules, standards, controls, advice, support etc. still needed? If so, in which areas?

	Need for more rules ←				→ No need for more rules
a) post-employment	☐	☐	☐	☐	☐
b) gift policies	☐	☐	☐	☐	☐
c) abusing organisational resources	☐	☐	☐	☐	☐
d) fraud	☐	☐	☐	☐	☐
e) corruption	☐	☐	☐	☐	☐
f) mobbing	☐	☐	☐	☐	☐
g) politicisation	☐	☐	☐	☐	☐
h) sexual intimidation	☐	☐	☐	☐	☐
i) public procurement	☐	☐	☐	☐	☐

Comments:

6. Assessing the costs, benefits and effectiveness of ethics systems

6.1 Have you ever evaluated the effectiveness of your ethics/integrity systems? If yes, what were the outcomes?

Comments:

6.2 Do you have evidence or estimates about the costs for monitoring ethics in ethics commissions, employment of staff, etc.? Are ethics-related costs increasing? Which instruments cause the highest costs? Are ethics policies cost-intensive or are they low cost?

Comments:

7. Final remarks

7.1 Do you have any plans or programmes in preparation to address ethical issues in your public service?

Comments:

7.2 What are the main issues and priorities (i.e. development challenges) concerning public-service ethics that your country needs to improve the most in the near future?

Comments:

7.3 Was something important ignored in this paper? Please give your additional comments.

Peter Lang · Internationaler Verlag der Wissenschaften

Christoph Demmke / Timo Moilanen

Civil Services in the EU of 27

Reform Outcomes and the Future of the Civil Service

Frankfurt am Main, Berlin, Bern, Bruxelles, New York, Oxford, Wien, 2010.
X, 285 pp., 14 fig., 47 tab.
ISBN 978-3-631-60466-3 · hardback € 54,95*

This volume compares and analyses the national civil services and the most important reform trends in the 27 Member States of the European Union. The authors first examine the reform processes concerning civil servants' legal status, organisational changes, recruitment policies, remuneration, decentralisation of human resource responsibilities, job security and ethics. They consider in what ways similarities and differences can be detected amongst the 27 Member States and whether and to what extent the national civil services move away from traditional bureaucratic structures. Finally, the authors discuss the main outcomes of the reform processes and the future of the classical civil service. This publication contrasts with the many popular and speculative statements that too often capture the headlines on the future of the civil service and the different human resource management reforms. Instead, it is a measured conclusion about emerging trends and developments in this important policy area. The authors argue that the reform of the public sector will not, as many have predicted, be characterised by clear changes and progress in the area. Instead, the outcomes of the reform reveal a more complex picture of piecemeal and paradoxical patterns of change.

Content: Civil Services · Human Resource Reforms · Comparative Public Services · Member States of the EU · Human Resource Management · Reform Outcomes

*The e-price includes German tax rate. Prices are subject to change without notice

Frankfurt am Main · Berlin · Bern · Bruxelles · New York · Oxford · Wien
Distribution: Verlag Peter Lang AG
Moosstr. 1, CH-2542 Pieterlen
Telefax 00 41 (0) 32 / 376 17 27
E-Mail info@peterlang.com

40 Years of Academic Publishing
Homepage http://www.peterlang.com

FSC
www.fsc.org
MIX
Papier | Fördert gute Waldnutzung
FSC® C083411

Kolibri 360 GmbH
Ferdinand-Jühlke-Straße 7
99095 Erfurt, Deutschland
produktsicherheit@kolibri360.de